The Aleph-Bet of Marriage

Journeying Toward Commitment

The Aleph-Bet of Marriage
Journeying Toward Commitment

Lynn Levy, C.S.W.

and the Department of Jewish Family Concerns
Union for Reform Judaism

URJ PRESS
FOR A LIFETIME OF JEWISH LEARNING

To Phil,

*whose love and commitment to our marriage
has been a model for so much of this work.*

Dear Couples,

You have made a commitment to one another that will enrich your lives beyond any measure. The Reform Jewish community respects and values such commitments and recognizes that each successful relationship brings a deeper spirituality to the couple, to their family, and to their community.

Before beginning this program, we want you to know that these workshops are the result of thorough studies and research that were conducted over a period of time. This program is committed to maintaining a nonjudgmental environment where, as a couple, you may begin to examine, discuss, and perhaps modify some of the techniques you will need to create a warm, loving, and lasting marital relationship that is inclusive of your Jewish heritage. Whether you have been raised in a Reform Jewish home, are new to the Jewish community or perhaps to liberal Judaism, or have been raised in another faith but are committed to a Jewish home, we believe this program will give you a fresh perspective and will speak to you in a way that you will find both relevant and enriching.

The tools and skills you gain will enable you to deal fairly and comfortably with one another. You are building the foundation of a partnership that will be at times challenging, exciting, and life-changing. We are committed to your success and wish to be part of the building of your foundation. It is our goal to enhance the cycles of your life together, enriching those experiences with the spirit and warmth of Jewish tradition.

L'shalom,

Rabbi Richard F. Address, D.Min.
Director, Department of Jewish Family
   Concerns

Lynn Levy, C.S.W.
Director, Premarital Education
Department of Jewish Family
   Concerns

Contents

Acknowledgments

The genesis for this program began at the 1999 Orlando Biennial when Rabbi Eric Yoffie, president of the Union of American Hebrew Congregations (UAHC), now the Union for Reform Judaism (URJ), proposed that we "assist engaged couples to consider issues of Jewish home life and child-rearing before their marriage takes place." A generous grant from the Charles and M. R. Shapiro Foundation in Chicago provided the impetus to begin this important work.

Great ideas are not born alone, but are the product of many seeds that have been planted along the way. This curriculum is no exception. To mention all who nurtured those seeds is difficult, but there are many to whom we extend deep gratitude: Rabbi Martin Wiener, president of the Central Conference of American Rabbis from 2001–2003, who planted seeds at every possible opportunity; Rabbi Paul Menitoff, executive vice president of the CCAR, for his deep commitment to the program and for assisting us in reaching rabbis across the North American continent; Rabbi David Fine, for being the first to facilitate a group long before it was a finished product, and his assistant, Cheryl Weight, for her extraordinary coordination of the first pilot site; Rabbi Jonathan Stein, Rabbi Martin Lawson, Rabbi Daniel Roberts, and Rabbi Harvey Winokur for their dedication to this project; Rabbi Nancy Wiener, Clinical Director of the Jacob and Hilda Blaustein Center for Pastoral Counseling at Hebrew Union College–Jewish Institute of Religion in New York, and Rabbi Richard Litvak for their insight and wisdom in helping us mold the direction of the core curriculum and for their clarity of vision.

Our lay leaders have given of themselves and their expertise without reservation. Thanks to Department of Jewish Family Concerns chair Jean Abarbanel and co-chairs Mike Grunebaum, Linda Wimmer, and Marshall Zolla; Premarital Committee chair Ginger Jacobs for her commitment and leadership to the process from its inception; Harriet Rosen for her writing skills, keen observations, and most of all, her friendship; John Hirsh and Herbert Leiman for keeping us sensitive to the issues for gay, lesbian, bisexual, and transgender couples; Jocelyn Dan Wurzburg and Stacey Chaikin for their insight from a legal perspective; and all the committee members, most especially Ann Wenger, for supporting us at every step of the way.

The feedback from the professional community—the social workers and psychologists who facilitated groups across the North American continent—was invaluable and led us to every new stage of development: Rabbi David Fine, Lee Pollak, Julie List, Cathy Bloomfield, and Gail Braverman. The Regional Coordinators acted as liaisons between the community, synagogues, and the URJ; Cheryl Weight, Ruth Goldberger, Val Scott, Meredith McDonald, Susanne Geshekter, Arlene Chernow, Raphael McGregor, and Neal Weiss led the way with their ability to coordinate and provide the necessary link between the community, synagogues, and rabbis. Much thanks to our colleagues at the URJ: Marcia Hochman for her understanding of true partnership and her never-ending acts of loving-kindness; Anthony Selvitella and Raphael McGregor for their constant support and assistance even when the whining got intolerable; Rabbi Lennard Thal, Rabbi Daniel Freelander, and Rabbi Elliot Kleinman for their commitment to strengthening the Reform Jewish family; Rabbi Hara Person and Ken Gesser at URJ Press for supporting this project and *Meeting at the Well*, so that they will be used by the community in partnership; and Rabbi Eric Yoffie for his extraordinary vision. Last, but certainly not least, most grateful appreciation to Rabbi Richard F. Address, Director of the Department of Jewish Family Concerns, for always being a model of true leadership and for his belief in the future of the Reform Jewish family. Without his guidance, *The Aleph-Bet of Marriage* would still be no more than an idea.

I am deeply grateful and feel blessed to have been given the opportunity to help bring premarital education to the Reform Jewish community. Those who will utilize this book and those who will direct the future of this program will continue on this sacred journey and will ensure the health and well-being of Reform Jewish families for generations to come. May you find fulfillment and a sense of purpose from this important work, as I have.

Some Basic Information

About Reading Text

- Many couples who participate in these groups come from diverse backgrounds that are reflective of their different cultures, levels of Jewish practice and observance, or different religions. This may be the first time you are reading Jewish text, and we would like to make the experience as interesting and nonthreatening as possible.

- Jewish text study provides a historical and theological basis for acts of self-care and mutual support. For many adults, knowing that they are continuing an age-old tradition bolsters their courage and enhances motivation. This is equally true for those with and without extensive formal Jewish education.

- Jewish text is complex, and as such, text study is complicated and can be anxiety inducing for some people. For the purposes of this program, all text will be translated into English.

- Text study should be denominationally appropriate and free of judgment, allowing for creative interpretation and individual connections with the texts. That being said, it is important to keep in mind that until recently all Jewish text, rabbinic stories, midrashim (the rabbinic stories that fill in the empty spaces of Torah), and their interpretations were written by and for men and reflect the times and culture in which they were written. Biblical and rabbinic texts are exclusive of egalitarian language or women's voices and reflect only heterosexual relationships. Therefore, any biblical stories that include courtships, encounters, and committed sexual relationships were written and spoken by men about men and women. There is great value and wisdom in these stories, and because Jewish thought has always stressed interpretation, we believe much can be gained from reading this material. As we acknowledge this past viewpoint, we want to stress that it does not reflect current understanding about gender and sexual orientation, nor is it reflective of a liberal Jewish perspective, one of inclusion and choice. Therefore, whenever possible, we have translated stories into more egalitarian language, but most traditional stories and texts will be told in their original forms. They will be interpreted in a broad and inclusive manner to offer insights to couples of all sexual orientations and to acknowledge the changed role and status of women.

- Successful use of traditional text is, in many ways, dependent on the removal of the notion that there is a "right" or "wrong" answer. The goal for the purposes of this program is to motivate and stimulate the implementation of a more sophisticated discussion model in which multiple "truths"—even those diametrically opposed—can coexist.

About the Language of Inclusion

Reform Judaism welcomes the participation of gay, lesbian, bisexual, and transgender Jews, and *The Aleph-Bet of Marriage* is designed for all couples who intend to make a lifetime commitment to one another and to create a Jewish home. In keeping with this policy of inclusion, every effort has been made in writing this program guide to use gender-neutral language whenever possible. We recognize that the definition of marriage is a contentious issue on the North American political scene, but our use of the word "marriage" in this program is not meant to exclude any committed couple, and our goal of successful Jewish families is the same for both heterosexual and same-sex couples.

About Participation in a Group

- Psycho-educational programs are learning opportunities. Participants can and will learn from the facilitator and one another if given the chance. "Practice makes perfect" is as true in this setting as it is in any other, yet participants should know that there is no such thing as a "perfect" interpersonal interaction or group.

- As in any learning experience, attendance, preparation, and participation will bring you the best results. Each pre-session and in-session exercise and reading has been selected to best fit the needs of your particular group. By your willingness to participate and to work seriously throughout this process, you not only enhance your own relationship, but you support the group's growth as well. In a shared experience, when everyone contributes, everyone gains. Please come prepared and help make this a rewarding experience for all who attend.

- Some issues trigger strong and emotional responses that may surprise, upset, or please you. This is quite normal. Please discuss your feelings with someone: either your partner, your workshop facilitator, a clinician, or your rabbi or cantor. While the purpose of the program is not group therapy, one of the goals of these sessions is to encourage you to explore some of the significant issues that contributed to shaping your personality, behaviors, and habits.

Exploring
Who You Are

Goals

- To gain a better understanding of self
- To explore families of origin
- To explore our expectations of marriage
- To gain a better understanding of how personality traits and factors affect the marriage
- To define Judaism's expectations for marriage

Text Study

(Note: Some translations have been reworded to reflect a modern and egalitarian interpretation. Please review the prior section entitled "Some Basic Information.")

In your reading of the following texts, consider what you think the writers had in mind and how you would apply it to your life in modernity.

> And the Eternal God said: It is not good that the man should be alone; I will make a partner for him.
>
> Genesis 2:18

> The wedding of the first couple was celebrated with pomp never repeated in the whole course of history, since God the Eternal, before presenting Eve to

Adam, attired and adorned her as a bride. Yea, God appealed to the angels, saying: "Come, let us perform services of friendship for Adam and his partner. . . ." The angels accordingly surrounded the marriage canopy, and God pronounced the blessings upon the bridal couple, as the *chazan* does under the *chuppah*. The angels then danced and played upon musical instruments before Adam and Eve in their bridal chambers.

Pirkei de D'Rabbi Eliezer
(Teachings of Rabbi Eliezer)

What is midrash? Midrash is a story or passage that explains something that is left unstated in Torah. There are many choices for couples in the role Judaism plays in your lives. This is a change from earlier times when there were more limited expectations from family and society. Exploring midrash offers an opportunity to interpret and reinterpret a story or passage's meaning in new ways and from our time's perspective. It provides a means to examine our lives and relationships within a liberal Jewish framework.

Where We Come from and Who We Are as Individuals

Read the following section as a prelude to the exploration of who you are as individuals and where you came from, in relation to your families of origin. You will also gain an awareness of Judaism's enduring understanding of the differences between individuals who marry, how they come together, and how they ultimately manage the joining of their lives.

We Are So Different. How Is It That People Marry?

Historically, people have married for a variety of reasons. Society has a profound impact on our choices of whether or not to marry. Throughout history, the reasons and methods related to marriage have varied tremendously and often were influenced by social and economic class differences.

In prebiblical and early biblical times, marriage was not a ceremonial rite of passage, accompanied by ritual; rather it was the custom for the bride and groom to be brought together by their parents and for dowry arrangements to be made and exchanged beforehand. The new couple having sexual intercourse for the first time officially sealed the marriage.

Isaac then brought her into the tent of his mother Sarah, and he took Rebekah as his wife. Isaac loved her, and thus found comfort after his mother's death.

Genesis 24:67

This is a beautiful reference describing when Isaac first meets his beloved Rebekah, chosen for him by his father Abraham's most trusted servant, Eliezer, from among Abraham's kinsmen.

In a midrash (*B'reishit Rabbah* 60:16) about this interaction, it is said that Isaac, seeing Rebekah for the first time, brings her to the tent of his deceased beloved mother. For the three years since her death, he has mourned for her constantly. Isaac finds comfort in his wife and no longer mourns for his mother.

The midrash makes a symbolic connection between Rebekah, his bride, and Sarah, his deceased mother. One hypothesis is that Isaac believes that his mother would have been pleased with his choice and so he takes Rebekah for his wife, finds comfort in her, and then loves her. The sequence of making a commitment to her, finding comfort in her, learning to love her, and finally, feeling comfort for his mother's death is not coincidental. The development of the relationship of Isaac and Rebekah is reflective of the biblical viewpoint that love develops over time, as partners share who they are, where they came from, and all that has contributed to the people they are at that moment in time.

Where Do You Come From?

This section will address:

- Who am I as an individual?
- Where am I coming from?
- What are the messages from my family of origin?
- How do these messages reflect my past and affect present relationships?
- How does this impact on my relationships?

Exercise 1. Creating Your Own Rituals

(Reprinted with permission from John Gottman and Nan Silver, *The Seven Principles for Making Marriage Work,* copyright 1999 by John M. Gottman,

Ph.D. and Nan Silver. Used by permission of Crown Publishers, a division of Random House, Inc.)

Do this exercise in dyads (pairs).

1. How do we or should we eat together at dinner? What is the meaning of dinnertime?

2. How should we part at the beginning of each day? What was this like in our families growing up? How should our reunions be?

3. How should bedtime be? What was it like in our families growing up?

4. What is the meaning of weekends? What were they like in our families growing up? What should they mean now?

5. What are our rituals about vacations? What were they like in our families growing up? What should they mean now?

6. Pick a meaningful holiday. What is the true meaning of the holiday to us? How should it be celebrated this year? How was it celebrated in each of our families growing up?

7. How do we each get refreshed and renewed? What is the meaning of these rituals?

8. What rituals do we have when someone is sick? What was this like in our families growing up? How should it be in our family?

You can build strong connections as a couple and a family through the creation of rituals. The following represent some suggestions of opportunities for the creation of rituals that can sanctify your private time together:

- A private, sacred space, such as Shabbat dinner for two.
- Celebrations of triumph—ways of celebrating almost any minor or major achievement and creating a culture of pride and praise in your marriage.

- Rituals surrounding bad luck, setbacks, fatigue, or exhaustion that help you support, heal, and renew yourselves.

- Rituals for entertaining friends, caring for other people in your community, or opening your home to others you care about.

- Rituals surrounding lovemaking and talking about it. These are important events that get left until the very end of the day when couples are exhausted. A ritual that makes you feel emotionally safe to talk about what is good and what needs improvement in lovemaking can be very helpful.

- Rituals for keeping in touch with relatives and friends. Family events and reunions can be planned.

- Birthdays and special events that recur. Examples are holidays of importance to you, religious celebration cycles, and anniversaries.

- Important rites of passage, such as *b'rit*, *b'nei mitzvah*, graduations, and weddings.

Exercise 2. Dinner with My Family

Do this exercise individually, and then share the answers with the group.

1. Who is at your dinner table?

2. How are they seated? Who is next to whom? Are these "regular" seats? What shape is the table? (Draw a picture, if you wish.)

3. Who is seated at the head of the table? Is this significant?

4. Who is responsible for preparing the meal? Does each member have a role?

5. Is dinner a meal that family members look forward to? Why or why not? Who is doing most of the talking? Is there any significance to this?

6. Who is doing the least talking? Is each family member given equal opportunity to share at mealtime?

7. Are there any distractions—dogs barking, TV on, phone ringing? What kind of conversation might be going on?

8. Is there fighting at the table? Why? Who instigates the fights? Who is the peacemaker? How does the meal end?

Exercise 3.   Mapping Your Relationship

This exercise encourages you to explore the history of your relationship. Do one or two of the following, as per instructions from your facilitator, as couples.

1. Discuss how the two of you met and got together. What was it about your intended that made him or her stand out? What were your first impressions of each other?

2. Describe what it was like when you were first dating. What were some of the big moments? How long was it before you decided to make a permanent commitment to one another? What were some of the tensions or concerns? If you are from different faiths, when did this first come up between you? Was it an issue?

3. Talk about how you decided to get married. How did you know this was "the one"? What went into the decision? Was it difficult or easy? How did you know you were in love? How did your family members respond?

4. Discuss your personal philosophies of marriage. What makes some marriages work and others not, in your opinion? Discuss the couples you know who are married, and decide whether they have a good or bad marriage. Which one, if any, would you like yours to resemble most?

5. Discuss your parents' marriages. Would you like to have a marriage like theirs, or would you like your own to be different?

Exercise 4. "Love Maps" Questionnaire

Please refer to Rabbi Daniel Judson and Rabbi Nancy Wiener, *Meeting at the Well*, chapter 2, "Make Me a Perfect Match."

(Reprinted with permission from John M. Gottman and Nan Silver, *The Seven Principles for Making Marriage Work*, copyright 1999 by John M. Gottman, Ph.D. and Nan Silver. Used by permission of Crown Publishers, a division of Random House, Inc.)

Do this exercise individually, and then score with the assistance of your facilitator.

1. I can name my partner's best friends. ____T ____F

2. I can tell you what stresses my partner is currently facing. ____T ____F

3. I know the names of some of the people who have been irritating my partner lately. ____T ____F

4. I can tell you some of my partner's life dreams. ____T ____F

5. I am very familiar with my partner's religious beliefs and ideas. ____T ____F

6. I can tell you about my partner's basic philosophy of life.   _____T   _____F

7. I can list the relatives my partner likes the least.   _____T   _____F

8. I know my partner's favorite music.   _____T   _____F

9. I can list my partner's three favorite movies.   _____T   _____F

10. My partner is familiar with my current stresses.   _____T   _____F

11. I know the three most special times in my partner's life.   _____T   _____F

12. I can tell you the most stressful thing that happened to my partner as a child.   _____T   _____F

13. I can list my partner's major aspirations and hopes in life.   _____T   _____F

14. I know my partner's major current worries.   _____T   _____F

15. My partner knows who my friends are.   _____T   _____F

16. I know what my partner would want to do if he or she won the lottery.   _____T   _____F

17. I can tell you in detail my first impressions of my partner.   _____T   _____F

18. Periodically I ask my partner about his or her world right now.   _____T   _____F

19. I feel that my partner knows me pretty well.   _____T   _____F

20. My partner is familiar with my hopes and aspirations.   _____T   _____F

Personality Traits

Commitment involves making the choice to give up some choices.

Scott Stanley, Ph.D.,
The Heart of Commitment

Who is rich? He who is satisfied with his portion.

Pirkei Avot 4:1

God created an imperfect world. This is a difficult concept for most people, but when you consider that many people are devoted to perfectionism, it may make more sense. We as human beings created in the divine image of God are constantly struggling with the issue of *tikkun olam,* repairing the world.

"I Love You, You're Perfect, Now Change . . ."

If you have not seen or heard of this off-Broadway musical revue, you can probably glean from the title the premise upon which it is based. We meet, become infatuated with the sheer perfection of our new partners, and proceed to fall in love. This point in the relationship is probably more suitably called the "honeymoon" than the actual honeymoon (which occurs at a time when both parties have just experienced an overwhelming amount of stress). It is at this point in the relationship that we think there is nothing we would want to change about our partners.

As time goes by, we begin to notice some of our partners' personality quirks, such as a particular way of dressing that seemed cute and enchanting at first, but now seems somewhat sophomoric. (He still wears his sweats to a nice restaurant! She dresses just a little too provocatively or inappropriately when we go to parties. My mom/dad never dressed like that/behaved like that!) The details may differ, but there is a moment in many relationships when one or the other partner realizes that his or her choice is not perfect! For some people, this may be a deal breaker, but for others, it may mean the beginning of a full-blown campaign to change the boyfriend/girlfriend.

From the outset, let us understand that substantively changing another person rarely works. At the heart of this desire may lie a desire for your partner to resemble you more closely. You cannot make your partner into a mirror image of yourself or into your idealized self. Your partner's basic personality and character were very much formed by the time you met and fell in love. People can change, but by and large, they do not change measurably, nor do they change because someone else wants them to change. Change only occurs when it is an identified desire on the part of the individual. If you truly have a gripe, we will explore how to request a change from your partner effectively.

Understanding, acknowledging, and accepting who you are and who your partner is will help you acclimate to your newly formed marital relationship and to accept lovingly the person you chose, with some of those quirks.

Exercise 5.   Who Am I?

(Reprinted with permission from John M. Gottman and Nan Silver, *The Seven Principles for Making Marriage Work,* copyright 1999 by John M. Gottman and Nan Silver. Used by permission of Crown Publishers, a division of Random House, Inc.)

Do this exercise individually, and then share in dyads.

My Triumphs and Strivings

1. What has happened in your life that you are particularly proud of? Write about your psychological triumphs, times when things went better than expected or periods when you emerged stronger from trials and tribulations. Include periods of stress and duress that you survived and mastered, small events that may still be of great importance to you, events from your childhood or the recent past, self-created challenges you met, periods when you felt powerful, glories and victories, wonderful friendships, and so on.

2. How have these successes shaped your life? How have they affected the way you think of yourself and your capabilities? How have they affected your goals and the things you strive for?

3. What role has pride (that is, feeling proud, being praised, expressing praise for others) played in your life? Did your parents show you that they were proud of you when you were a child? How? How have other people responded to your accomplishments?

4. Did your parents show you that they loved you? How? Was affection readily expressed in your family? If not, what are the effects and implications of this for your marriage?

5. What role does pride in your accomplishments play in your marriage? What role do your own personal goals have in your marriage? What do you want your partner to know and understand about your past, present, and future plans? How do you show pride in one another?

My Injuries and Healings

1. What difficult events or periods have you gone through? Write about any significant psychological insults and injuries you have sustained as well as your

losses, disappointments, trials, and tribulations. Include periods of stress, despair, hopelessness, and loneliness. Also include any deep traumas you underwent as a child or adult, such as harmful relationships, humiliating events, molestation, abuse, rape, or torture.

2. How did you survive these traumas? What are their lasting effects on you?

3. How did you strengthen and heal yourself? How did you redress your grievances? How did you revive and restore yourself?

4. How did you gird and protect yourself against this ever happening again?

5. How do these injuries and the ways you protect and heal yourself affect your marriage today? What do you want your partner to know and understand about these aspects of your self?

My Emotional World

1. How did your family express the following when you were a child:

   Anger?

   Sadness?

   Fear?

   Affection?

   Interest in one another?

2. During your childhood, did your family have to cope with a particular emotional problem, such as aggression between parents, a depressed parent, or a parent who was somewhat emotionally wounded? What implications does this have for your marriage and your other close relationships to friends, parents, siblings, and children?

3. What is your own philosophy about expressing feelings, particularly sadness, anger, fear, pride, and love? Are any of these difficult for you to express or see expressed by your partner? What is the basis of your philosophy?

4. What differences exist between you and your partner in the area of expressing emotion? What is behind these differences? What are the implications of these differences for you?

My Mission and Legacy

1. Imagine that you are standing in a graveyard looking at your own tombstone. Write the epitaph you would like to see there. Begin with the words "Here lies. . . ."

2. Write your own obituary. How do you want people to think of your life, to remember you?

3. Now you're ready to write a mission statement for your own life. What is the purpose of your life? What is its meaning? What are you trying to accomplish? What is your larger struggle?

4. What legacy would you like to leave when you die?

5. What significant goals have you yet to realize? Minor examples are learning to play the banjo, climbing a mountain, and so on.

Who I Want to Become

Take a moment to reflect on what you have just written. We are all involved in becoming the person we most want to be. In that struggle we all have demons to fight and overcome.

1. Describe the person you want to become.

2. How can you best become that person?

3. What struggles have you already faced in trying to become that person?

4. What demons have you had to fight or still have to fight?

5. What would you most like to change about yourself?

6. What dreams have you denied yourself or failed to develop?

7. What do you want your life to be like in five years?

8. What is the story of the kind of person you would like to be?

At-Home Exercises

What follows are a contination of the "Who Am I?" exercises and a "Blessing Exercise." Please complete them at home prior to the next session. Give yourselves the gift of enough time to think and work through your answers.

Who Am I? (continued)

Briefly answer the following questions separately; then share them together.

1. What are your values? Are they consistent with the values you learned in your family of origin? If not, where did they come from?

2. Do you feel your partner shares your values? Are they the same values shared by your family of origin?

3. How did your family of origin express emotion? Give examples that illustrate the expression of joy, fear, anger, sadness, etc.

4. Describe the structure of your family of origin. Who was the dominant figure in your family? Can you describe your relationship with your siblings? What about your siblings and your parents? If you are an only child, how did this affect the structure of your family?

5. Describe the family you hope to be creating. How will that family be similar to or different from your family of origin?

6. Describe the holiday celebrations from your family of origin. What are your warmest memories? Which memories are best forgotten?

7. Describe how you envision holiday celebrations with the family you will be creating. How will they be similar to or different from those you experienced as a child?

8. Describe how your family members reacted to your choice of partner. Has the relationship changed over time? Are you satisfied with the current status of the relationship?

9. What are your fears and/or fantasies about your interactions as a couple with your family of origin? If you are an interfaith couple or a same sex couple, will this affect the family dynamics? To what extent? Have you discussed how you will address these issues in the relationship?

10. What was the message in your family of origin about dealing with extended
    family members and in-laws? How will this impact on your own decisions
    regarding extended family members and in-laws?

בָּרוּךְ אַתָּה, יְיָ אֱלֹהֵינוּ, מֶלֶךְ הָעוֹלָם, בּוֹרֵא פְּרִי הַגָּפֶן.

Baruch atah, Adonai Eloheinu, Melech haolam, borei p'ri hagafen.

Blessed are You, *Adonai* our God, Ruler of the universe, Creator of the fruit
of the vine.

                                  First of the Seven Blessings *(Sheva B'rachot)*

The most common Jewish prayer is the *b'rachah*, the blessing. Blessings are central to Jewish life and are designed to help us see the sacred in all we encounter
in the world. Blessings add special meaning to even the most mundane encounter.
All blessings begin with the same words: *Baruch atah, Adonai Eloheinu, Melech
haolam . . .* (translated as: "Blessed are You, *Adonai,* our God, Ruler of the universe"). After that, the endings change according to the situation.

This prayer is the first of the *Sheva B'rachot.* You may recognize that it is also the
prayer that we say over wine on Shabbat eve and other festive occasions. It can
be interpreted as an expression of our gratefulness for having the ability to use
the grapes for such divine purpose as a sweet wine that enhances our meals, but
it may also be interpreted as a reminder of the sweetness of the occasion, and the
beginning of your life together.

We know how blessed you feel to have found one another, to be standing on the
threshold of an exciting time in your lives. We encourage you to give a voice to
these emotions of gratitude and participate in the following exercise of "counting
your blessings."

Blessing Exercise

Take the time to write a blessing that reflects how you feel about being at this
stage of your life. The blessing should either acknowledge your gratitude for your
loved one, the romance in your life, or simply be an opportunity to share in an
expression that reflects the beauty of the moment.

Communicating

Goals

- To look at communication through Jewish eyes
- To define communication and to focus on the communication styles of each partner
- To explore the way communication patterns work
- To understand principles of communication
- To define rules for effective communication
- To put into practice effective methods of communication

Text Study: A Look at Communicating through Jewish Eyes

Jewish tradition teaches that improper speech can be more damaging than improper action. The Torah story of ten spies who sinned by speaking evil about the Land of Israel (Numbers 13–14) shows the consequences of the spies' words for the former slaves who had come out of Egypt.

Because they accepted the spies' words, the freed Jews were prevented from being the generation to inherit the Land. Instead, it was their fate to wander for forty years in the desert and die without ever entering the land God had promised.

The Talmud further states that the physiological makeup of the human body demonstrates how the tongue must be guarded. Other limbs of our bodies are exposed, but the tongue is hidden, protected by the mouth and the teeth, to prevent misuse (Babylonian Talmud, _B'rachot_ 17a). In short, Jewish text teaches us that "words can kill."

One of the principal differences between humans and all other creatures is a human being's ability to articulate intelligent thought. Words have tremendous power; they communicate with both symbolic and literal meaning.

There is great emphasis placed on how a Jew uses speech. The damage caused by speaking evil is often more pronounced and permanent than a physical blow. While a physical injury will heal, a person rarely recuperates from the effects of evil speech, even after an extended time period. That is why the traditional Jewish punishment for publicly embarrassing someone with words is much more severe than the punishment for physically hurting another individual.

Jewish tradition informs us of the benefits of treating one's partner with respect and dignity. Marks of distinction are accorded to those individuals who display respect, both mutual and self-respect, and to those who honor all human beings. Are we always careful to convey what we *really* mean in way that will be understood?

There are many other teachings on these ideas:

> Let your friend's honor be as dear as your own.
>
> *Pirkei Avot* 2:15

> Who is honored? One who honors fellow humankind.
>
> *Pirkei Avot* 4:1

> Do not despise any fellow human being.
>
> *Pirkei Avot* 4:3

> Cherish the honor of your student as your own.
>
> *Pirkei Avot* 4:15

> Whoever promotes his own honor at the expense of his neighbor's degradation has no share in the world-to-come.
>
> *B'reishit Rabbah*

> Throw yourself into a blazing furnace rather than shame a fellow human being in public.
>
> Babylonian Talmud, *B'rachot* 43b

> God grant that you neither shame nor be shamed.
>
> Babylonian Talmud, *Mo-eid Katan* 9b

Effective Communication

Good communication skills increase your ability to get what you want and what you need from situations or interactions. You might be familiar with the elements of the method we will be using for this program. The emphasis is on ownership of one's words. The concept is very simple: once you have said something, it remains there as a reminder of what is either right or wrong between the two of you. What we will address is the common misuse of words, leading to frequent miscommunication.

As you work through the important issues in your relationship, this method will help you communicate clearly and will support the environment of trust and respect you both wish to build. Let's first look at what your current style of communication is and how well it works for you. As you learn this method, you may wish to try it in the workplace and with parents, friends, and other family members. You should see positive feedback coming your way.

Exercise 6.   What Kind of a Communicator Are You?

Do this exercise individually, and then share the answers with the group.

1. What were the messages about communication you received as a child?

2. What were the messages you received from parents, teachers, grandparents, and friends about communication?

3. Do you become angry quickly, escalating a simple discussion to an argument?

4. After whom do you model your style of communication? Is there one person whose style you admired? Disliked?

5. Are you satisfied with the results you get from your current style of communication?

Some Principles of Communication

Every couple will experience some differences of opinion in their relationship. That is good and normal. It is how you approach these differences and, ultimately, how you resolve them that is truly important and will impact on your ability to communicate in your marriage. It is important that you do not interpret differences of opinion to mean that your partner disapproves of you, rejects you as a person, or will betray you because of your differing beliefs. Rather, these differences of opinion ultimately will allow you and your partner to grow closer. Together, you can learn how best to communicate your needs and feelings, and that will bring you to a new level of intimacy. Use the following principles of communication as your guide:

- BE OPEN TO YOUR DIFFERENCES. As you discovered from the last session, your background and your life experiences greatly determine what your opinions and strongly held beliefs are at this time in your life. Struggles in your relationship will not occur because of your differing beliefs, but rather out of an inability to tolerate and accept as different an opinion that is not your own.

- THERE IS NO ONE RIGHT ANSWER. This is, perhaps, the most important principle to remember in communication, and this is a difficult one for most people to accept. As adults, we have to accept that there are many issues about which people hold widely different views—not wrong ones, but differing ones.

  You have only to hear a political debate to understand that each issue can be viewed and interpreted on a variety of levels and from a myriad of perspectives. Though you may not be a believer now, we hope you will come to value and, quite possibly, incorporate one another's viewpoints into your understanding of any given topic or situation.

- BE OPEN . . . YOUR OPINIONS COUNT, even though you are now part of a couple. No one wants you to relinquish your personal ideas or opinions. In part, they are what distinguish you from other people, and they are your own. BUT, combativeness can become habitual, and you may not even notice it.

  When you feel that there is something you need to communicate, think about it first. Ask yourself, "How important is this point I am about to make? Am I making a point just to be heard or is it truly important?" Get in touch with your underlying needs and feelings before you bring something up. You may be displacing feelings onto this issue.

- DON'T DEVELOP A "LAUNDRY LIST." A "laundry list" contains grievances that have been stored up. Some people do this without realizing it, but others wait until there is enough ammunition to win their point. This is not constructive or helpful to the relationship. If you really have a grievance, air it when it arises. It has much more credibility, and your partner will be more receptive to hearing what you have to say.

BEWARE!

There are attitudes and behaviors that you may have learned that can prevent effective communication. Beware of the following common communication pitfalls:

Critical or judgmental behavior

Sarcasm, contempt, antagonism, arrogance

Defensiveness

Game-playing and manipulative behavior

Controlling style

Placating or self-deprecating behavior

Behaving in a superior way

Each of these behaviors used either alone or in conjunction with another can sabotage effective communication. Often, more than one of these problems may occur at the same time. You may not even be aware that you are exhibiting any of these behaviors, but take a minute and reflect on how you may be being perceived. Better yet, ask your partner!

Rules for Effective Communication

- LISTEN WITH YOUR FULL ATTENTION. This means that you have set aside enough time to focus on what your partner has to say. You should not be doing anything that will distract you, such as reading a book, watching television, taking phone calls, or playing with pets.

- DO NOT MAKE JUDGMENTS WHILE YOUR PARTNER IS SPEAKING. Try to allow your partner to finish speaking before you formulate your rebuttal.

- TAKE TURNS. Allow your partner his/her fair share of time to speak. Agree on a reasonable amount of time for each person to speak (for example, fifteen minutes).

- KEEP THE MESSAGE SIMPLE. This is important and also difficult, since it is the practice of many people to store information to be used against a partner in future conversations. If you stockpile, your message will not be heard.

The simpler, the better. Each interaction should be viewed as a personal message intended only for your partner.

- CHECK IN WITH YOUR PARTNER, OR ASK FOR CLARIFICATION TO MAKE SURE YOU ARE INTERPRETING/DELIVERING THE MESSAGE ACCURATELY. Too often, we think we have accurately understood our partner's message, but we really have misinterpreted all or part of the message.

- TRY TO KEEP YOUR TONE AND YOUR BODY LANGUAGE SIMPLE. Sometimes our tone and mannerisms belie our messages, which could lead to confusion. Always try to show love and respect when sharing your thoughts with your partner, especially if the information is of a difficult nature.

- QUESTIONS ARE NOT ALWAYS JUST QUESTIONS. We often use questions as accusations, such as, "When will you be home?" This question can really mean "I'd like to know when to plan on dinner," or "You've been late every night this week, and I'm angry at you." These hidden/implicit messages can trigger defensiveness in your partner, which, in turn, can lead to miscommunication.

  If you are angry, it is best to make an honest statement, such as, "I'm upset because you haven't phoned the last few times you were late." Or, if you are just seeking information, how about, "I'd like to know what time to plan on dinner. Do you have any idea what time you might be home?"

  Phrasing your questions and feelings this way may seem contrived to you at first, but it prevents a lot of miscommunications and misinterpretations that could lead to anger, hurt feelings, and unnecessary conflict.

- BE RESPECTFUL OF YOUR PARTNER. You may not understand why your partner is upset about something, or even think that it is foolish, but never take your partner's feelings lightly. You destroy trust when you belittle a person's feelings. Remember that you are different people, and the same things are not going to make you happy or upset you, so be respectful.

- TAKE YOUR PARTNER'S SIDE. Whenever possible, support your partner when he or she shares information of a sensitive nature, such as problems at work or difficulties with a parent, sibling, or friend. If you disagree with your partner's position, try to find an area where you do agree or where you can be supportive. Empathize with your partner's feelings or frustrations by saying things such as, "It sounds like that must have been hard for you," or "You seem really upset by the situation," or "I know how hard you worked on that project." Saying something that indicates you are on your partner's side will make it easier to hear if there are points upon which you may disagree.

- DON'T OFFER ADVICE UNLESS IT IS REQUESTED. If you feel you must share your thoughts, ask if it is the right time for your partner to hear some thoughts you have. If your partner responds negatively, wait for the right moment to bring it up again, or do not bring it up again at all. Some people feel they have not been truly helpful unless they have solved the problem for their loved one. If you feel you must offer something, just offer your support by staying interested in the outcome of the issue. Perhaps checking in with your partner on this unresolved issue in a day or two, without trying to "fix it," would feel helpful.

- GIVE YOUR PARTNER THE BENEFIT OF THE DOUBT. If you have a grievance or issue that has been bothering you, begin the communication with a positive statement. Don't assume your partner's intention was to hurt your feelings or behave in a way that you find uncomfortable. Assure your partner that you know his or her heart must have been in the right place. It is always easier to hear the negative once we have been reassured of the love and good intentions of the bearer.

Exercise 7. Case Study

Read this exercise individually, and then follow the instructions of the facilitator.

Background

Alex is a thirty-two-year-old Jewish man living in a major urban center near the suburban community in which he grew up. His parents still live in the house where he was born and where they raised their three boys. They describe themselves as "upper middle class" and feel they gave as much as they could to their children, both emotionally and financially. Now, it is "their" time.

They travel quite a bit but are always home for the Jewish holidays, ready to celebrate with their sons and their families, though they describe themselves as "not terribly committed Jews." The holidays are seen as a time for the family to get together. They have not belonged to a synagogue since Alex was a bar mitzvah and do not plan to join one in the future.

Alex is the only unmarried sibling. His two brothers married Jewish girls, and each have a child, both girls. His parents do not baby-sit. They say it is "not their thing." Alex is the youngest, and he feels very close to his parents and sees their relationship as a role model. They share the same interests and are each other's best friends.

Alex has looked for a long time for the "right" girl to bring home to his family. He knows he has found this in Tracey. That is why he feels comfortable bringing her into his apartment and sharing his space with her. It feels "right" to him, and now they can save some money for the future.

Tracey is twenty-eight years old. She grew up in a small town, far from an urban center. She went to a large university and decided that, despite the fact that she loved her parents and her brother, she would move one day to a city where she could pursue her chosen career as a publicist.

Tracey's family belongs to a Conservative synagogue, where her father was president of the men's club and her mother was a member of the board of trustees. Tracey says that in her community, you had to "make a real effort to feel the least bit Jewish." Both her parents were raised in homes where Judaism was important to their lives, and they celebrated Shabbat with a special dinner and family rituals every week.

Since moving away, she has really missed Shabbat and even joined a synagogue as a "single." She met Alex at a lecture on Israel at her synagogue. He attended with a friend of his, and they instantly connected. After going out for coffee, they both knew they would see a lot more of each other.

Tracey was a bit surprised when he confided in her that being Jewish was not all that important to him. It was more important to "be a good person," he said. She did not make mention of her own feelings toward being Jewish but invited him to Shabbat dinner at her cozy apartment, where she cooked him a traditional meal and lit candles and said the prayers. He told her he thought it was "cute" that she did that. He helped her with the dishes and read to her from her favorite book of poetry.

Tracey believed they had incredibly similar likes and dislikes. She knew they were headed in a good direction. He reminded her of her brother Mike physically. They were both tall and good-looking, but Alex was so much like her dad in his kindness. He was a truly kind person.

Their Issues

Alex and Tracey have been dating for the past three and a half years. They decided to get married about six months ago and felt that they could save some money before the wedding, which was one year away, if they shared an apartment.

Tracey always felt that she did not want to move in together, that it would diminish the excitement and what she felt was so special about making this sacred commitment to one another, but Alex was very convincing in his appeal for putting some money away before their marriage.

Alex felt, since his was the larger of the two apartments and was well located to both their jobs, that Tracey should forfeit her apartment and move into Alex's space. Alex had furnished the apartment as a "bachelor's pad" with furniture from his parents' house and "stuff" he had accumulated over the past few years.

Though Tracey felt he had done a good job, "adequate for a guy living alone," in her words, the décor did not reflect Tracey's own style. This, of course, was not directly conveyed to Alex, as Tracey felt she did not want to offend him or hurt his feelings regarding furniture he may have chosen or taken from his mom and dad's home. So, instead, she decided to move in and let time work through her feelings.

Tracey thought that perhaps she would not feel so bad once she and Alex were living together. After all, he was everything she ever wanted in a mate. He was tall and handsome, had an MBA from a prestigious university, had a job that promised to earn him respect and a very good salary, was a hard worker, and was very kind.

These were important traits to Tracey. She was lucky. Based on the men that her friends were meeting, she felt that Alex was a good catch, and she knew they would have a good life together. She felt somewhat disappointed that his parents were not more "involved" and secretly knew she would miss the warmth and feeling of connectedness of her own family and their Shabbat dinners.

What brings them for help at this juncture is that Tracey has been, according to Alex, "pulling away." She mopes around the apartment, when she is there, but mostly she finds reasons not to be at home. She does not take an interest in the apartment and has been acting "strangely" since she moved in.

When Alex was asked how much of Tracey's belongings are in his apartment, he responded, "Her clothes—all of them and that is a lot—and pictures of her family. Oh, and her Shabbat candlesticks." Tracey appeared on the verge of tears as he made this recitation.

It was obvious that Tracey was feeling unhappy without some of her belongings, and when asked about her feelings, she answered, "I feel like a visitor—a welcome visitor, but a guest, nonetheless." Alex was surprised to hear this and acknowledged that it was the first inkling he had of Tracey's feelings. He never meant to hurt her, but he thought it all had made perfect, logical sense.

בָּרוּךְ אַתָּה, יְיָ אֱלֹהֵנוּ, מֶלֶךְ הָעוֹלָם, שֶׁהַכֹּל בָּרָא לִכְבוֹדוֹ.

Baruch atah, Adonai Eloheinu, Melech haolam, shehakol bara lichvodo.

We praise You, *Adonai* our God, Ruler of the universe, You created all things for Your glory.

Second of the Seven Blessings *(Sheva B'rachot)*

At-Home Exercise: Blessing Exercise

Write a blessing that reflects your feelings and/or gratitude for the openness of your communication, for being able to share your deepest thoughts and feelings with your partner.

Fighting Fair

Goals

- To assess your history of fighting

- To help you discover what makes you angry

- To help you learn to analyze a problem

- To gain a better understanding of what your communication obstacles are and to develop strategies for overcoming these obstacles

- To learn and practice the skill of "fair fighting"

- To become familiar with your and your partner's weak spots and to learn to navigate them with sensitivity

Text Study: On Making Marriages

The following story is a well-known midrash. In a theological discussion with Rabbi Yosei ben Chalafta regarding the whereabouts of God, a wealthy Roman matron challenged the rabbi in this way. She conceded that God was the almighty Creator, but she then asked the rabbi, "Now that the world is created, what is there left for God to do?"

"Among other things," answered the rabbi, "God arranges marriages, and facilitates the adjustment between husbands and wives."

"What a trivial task to monopolize the efforts of an omnipotent God!" she scoffed. "I can do the same job more easily. I have a number of male and female slaves, and in a single hour I can pair them all off."

"It may appear easy to you," said the rabbi, "yet every marriage is as diffi-cult for God as was the parting of the Red Sea." Rabbi Yosei went his way.

And what did the matron do? She called together a thousand male and a thousand female slaves, arranged them in rows, and said, "This one will marry this one, and this one will marry this one," until she had paired them all off in a single night.

The next morning, they came to her—this one's arm broken and this one's eye blackened, another one's leg broken. "What happened?" she asked. One said, "I don't want her." And the other cried, "I don't want him." The matron immediately sent for Rabbi Yosei and said to him, "Rabbi, your Torah is true and exalted, and everything you spoke you spoke well."

B'reishit Rabbah 68:4

To join in wedlock as husband and bride is as hard as it was to divide the Red Sea.

Babylonian Talmud, *Sotah* 2a

Exercise 8.   Assessing Your History and Skills of Fighting

How you view yourself and what you think is your style as a fighter is important to your relationship. Equally important is how your partner views your style.

Examine and assess your fighting skills by writing down:

1. What things you fight about

2. How your style of fighting resembles conflicts in your own family background

By looking at these two factors, you may realize that what you're fighting with your partner about really has little or nothing to do with your partner, but may reflect more what difficulties you have had historically with others in your life. It is important to be able to ascertain what is "historical" and what is happening in the "here and now."

Flooding

Sometimes people experience feelings that overwhelm them. This response is called "flooding." Feeling flooded is not uncommon, and there are different triggers for each person. At those flooded moments, an individual can feel unfairly attacked, misinterpreted, misunderstood, or righteously indignant. Responses differ. Some people will feel like running away, others like striking back, and still others will be so emotionally overwhelmed they do not know how to respond. Some may even experience physical symptoms, such as difficulty breathing, hot flashes, muscular tension, headaches, or a racing heart.

When you are feeling flooded, the first thing you want to do is stop the interaction and calm yourself down. This may mean taking a time-out or just walking away for a few minutes, and then resuming the interaction.

The following exercise will help you look at those things that result in your feeling flooded and what blocks the road toward good communication.

Exercise 9. Flooding

(Reprinted with permission from John Gottman and Nan Silver, *Why Marriages Succeed or Fail,* copyright 1994, by Fireside, a division of Simon & Schuster.)

To help uncover some of the roadblocks to good communication and to discover whether flooding is a significant problem in your relationship, answer the following questions individually, and then score with the assistance of the facilitator.

1. Our discussions get too heated.   ____T ____F

2. I have a hard time calming down.   ____T ____F

3. One of us is going to say something we will regret.   ____T ____F

4. My partner gets too upset.   ____T ____F

5. After a fight I want to keep my distance.   ____T ____F

6. My partner yells unnecessarily.   ____T ____F

7. I feel overwhelmed by our arguments.   ____T ____F

8. I can't think straight when my partner gets hostile.   ____T ____F

9. Why can't we talk more logically?   ____T ____F

10. My partner's negativity often comes out of nowhere.   ____T ____F

11. There's often no stopping my partner's temper.   ____T ____F

12. I feel like running away during our fights.   ____T ____F

13. Small issues suddenly become big ones.   ____T ____F

14. I can't calm down very easily during an argument.   ____T ____F

15. My partner has a long list of unreasonable demands.   ____T ____F

What Are Some of the Obstacles to Fighting Fair?

Any of the following styles can impede the process of good communication, fighting fair, and problem solving. Each, in their own way, leads to misunderstanding and misinterpretation and tends to have a message and a motive of its own:

- Screaming and yelling
- Physical and mental abuse
- Withdrawing—the "silent treatment"
- Withdrawing physically
- Crying or tearful pleas
- Uninvolved, distracted, and/or inattentive behavior
- Acting super-rational with an air of superiority
- Ridiculing, judging, criticizing
- Placating or acting compliant to keep the peace
- Needing to be "right"
- Holding on to old, angry feelings

Principles for Fighting Fairly

Learn them and use them!

- USE "I" STATEMENTS AND AVOID "YOU" STATEMENTS. It puts your partner on the defensive if you start your sentence with "you."

- USE "HEART" STATEMENTS AND AVOID "HEAD" STATEMENTS. Tell your partner how you feel and not what you think. When you do this, you are saying that your feelings are your own and you have a right to them . . . and that you shouldn't be judged for them.

- DO NOT INTERRUPT. LISTEN, LISTEN, LISTEN. . . . This is difficult, but very important. You message will be: "I will not only 'hear' you, but will truly 'listen' to you and will try to understand your point of view without rushing in with my own thoughts and views." Only then can your partner "hear" and "listen" to you.

- DO NOT "DEPERSONALIZE" THE FIGHT. This is about you and your partner. Maintain eye contact at all times. Stop whatever else you may be doing (like watching TV). Do not name-call or trivialize your or your partner's feelings by making a joke of them. Sit down and talk it through. Do not walk out unless you both agree you need a "time out" to cool down. Treat each other with dignity and respect.

- FIGHT WITH LOVE. LOVE IS WHAT BINDS YOU. Remember! Even in anger and rage, you love one another. Do not say anything that will belittle or destroy the relationship. Relationships are fragile and must be treated with sensitivity and nurturing.

- KEEP IT NEAT AND SIMPLE. Try to stick to the agenda and issue at hand. Keep the message simple, and try to address your feelings honestly and succinctly. If you find it hard to communicate, start off by saying, "I feel angry [or hurt] when . . . ." This will make it easier to target the issue. Express to your partner how difficult this kind of conversation is for you. Please remember to be patient with each other.

- DON'T PLAY "MIND" OR "HEAD" GAMES. REMEMBER! YOU LOVE ONE ANOTHER. Try to be direct, honest, and sincere—this is the person you love and with whom you have chosen to spend the rest of your life. Don't play games or try to fool each other. You will be damaging the foundation of your relationship—TRUST AND HONESTY.

- ASK FOR WHAT YOU NEED! Your partner cannot read your mind, so be prepared to have to ask for what you need if you feel your needs are not being met. It is important for couples to understand that a requirement of a successful partnership is the ability to take responsibility for identifying your needs from the partnership and asking appropriately that those needs be met, assuming these are reasonable needs.

- DON'T ABUSE ONE ANOTHER. You know things about your partner that no one else may know. You know what topics are sensitive and difficult for each other. You know each other's weak spots. Do not abuse this knowledge by "hitting below the belt." Instead, you should agree that there are topics and lines that you will not cross, such as comparing your partner's negative behavior to that of his/her mother, father, or sibling. One of the by-products of intimacy is vulnerability. Create a safe environment for you and your partner to share and grow together. Guard it with your life and for the future of your marriage!

- IF THERE IS A TIME WHEN INTERVENTION IS CALLED FOR, SEEK PROFESSIONAL HELP. The nine points above provide good information, but if these tips are not adequate to deal with your fighting patterns, don't wait. Find help quickly. Severe problems tend to become worse, not better. Look for these signs to determine if you need professional help:

  - If you feel you are fighting too frequently and are not able to resolve the conflicts.

  - If your feelings of anger and hurt are increasing in intensity.

  - If there is physical or mental abuse.

Skills Practicing—Scenario

Melissa and Jonathan are a couple aged twenty-five and twenty-seven, respectively. They have lived together for the past seven months after dating for three and a half years. They are both working at high-powered jobs, she as a financial analyst and he as an attorney in a large corporate law firm in a large city. Since they both work long hours, they felt that living together would provide more time together and would, thereby, make things a little less "stressful." They both report that their "dates" had become more of a battling ground than an opportunity to share intimate time together. Both Melissa and Jonathan felt the reason for this was the way their lives were structured around their work. Neither felt they could make changes in this area, as they were both building careers that were important to them on a variety of levels.

When Melissa and Jonathan first came for help with their fighting, they talked a lot about how the other person "missed the point." Jonathan would say, "You see, Melissa just doesn't see anyone else's point of view. She just wants things done her way. She expects everyone to just conform to her way of doing things." Melissa, for her part, said, "Jonathan has been babied his whole life. His mother and sisters have made him feel like a prince, and he does not like the fact that I do not want to cater to all his whims, all the time. I want him to understand that I have needs in this relationship also. It's not that I do not see his point of view, I just don't agree with it. And I am not going to do something his way just because he wants me to."

Melissa and Jonathan were clearly at an impasse. They had hit a wall. When we started our discussions, they did not have a particular issue that was bothering them, but complained of general things as stated above. There was more going on here. They said they really loved one another, and when they could stop bickering, there was no one else either one would rather be with. Jonathan enjoyed Melissa's sense of humor, her intellect, and the way she looked. Melissa said Jonathan was the most highly spirited, intelligent, and super-honest person she had ever met, and he was sexy. It appeared that they wanted to find a way to get over some of these issues.

We talked a lot about Melissa's family, her parents' marriage, what she considered good and not so good from their union. She discussed her relationship with her siblings, in particular her older sister, who seemed to get a good share of the attention and forced Melissa to be her "slave," as she put it. Jonathan talked a great deal about his mother and sisters. His parents had divorced when he was only six years old, and his father had moved across the country when he remarried and had another family. He saw his father once a year at no particular time or holiday, whenever they could find time to fit it in. He said that was OK with him because he had such a strong relationship with his mother and sisters. There is a six-year age difference between him and his youngest sister and eight years between the eldest and him. He said he did feel very "special" growing up and felt it contributed to his ability to be successful. Neither Melissa nor Jonathan had a strong insight into what their fights were about, but felt they needed to figure out how to manage them or they would have to break up, which neither wanted to do.

בָּרוּךְ אַתָּה, יְיָ אֱלֹהֵינוּ, מֶלֶךְ הָעוֹלָם, יוֹצֵר הָאָדָם.

Baruch atah, Adonai Eloheinu, Melech haolam yotzer haadam.

We praise you, *Adonai* our God, Ruler of the universe, Creator of humanity.

Third of the Seven Blessings *(Sheva B'rachot)*

At-Home Exercises

Blessing Exercise

By using compromise and positive communication skills, you bring blessings to your home and to the ways you mediate disagreements between you and family members. Create a blessing for things that compel you to do loving deeds, to seek peace in the world and at home.

Companionship/Fun and Activity

Answer the following questions individually, and bring them to next week's session.

1. Who will be primarily responsible for maintaining the social life within the relationship? How will you find time for the people in your life?

2. Who are the important people in your life?

3. How will you decide where and how to spend leisure time?

4. How will you decide how much money should be allocated to leisure time?

5. What are some of the activities that are important to you? To your partner?

6. How will you determine how much time will be spent on leisure activities? How will you find the time for those activities?

7. Who will be responsible for the planning of vacations?

The Art of Negotiating

Goals

- To acquire the skills necessary to analyze differences
- To use your understanding of individual fighting styles and your strengthened communication skills to negotiate your differences
- To learn a new format and method for renegotiating your marital contract
- To practice this new format

Text Study

Negotiation is not new to Judaism. The very basis of our talmudic tradition rests on the concept of discussion, debate, and negotiation.

There were two great schools of talmudic study, *Beit Hillel* and *Beit Shammai*, each staunchly holding to their own interpretation of Torah. These two academies were rivals and in a constant state of debate on a variety of issues.

Because talmudic debates are based on the need to arrive at essential truths, scholars refused to be cowed by the brilliance of an argument if it was unfounded and were determined to examine the evidence.

Beit Hillel was deemed preferable over *Beit Shammai* because this school first repeated *Beit Shammai*'s point of view on any given subject before offering its own position. This great tradition models tolerance for different beliefs and gives validity and credibility to the feelings of others.

The art of negotiation is perhaps best seen from a Jewish perspective through the symbol of the mezuzah, which is attached to the doorpost of a Jewish home. The slanting of the mezuzah is the result of a difference of opinion between Rashi and his grandson Rabbi Jacob ben Meir, known as Rabbenu Tam.

According to Rashi, the mezuzah should be attached vertically, but according to Rabbenu Tam, it should be in a horizontal position. As a compromise, it has become customary to put it up slantwise. It is wonderful that the symbol that best exemplifies the beginning of a new Jewish home is also the result of a meaningful negotiation.

The Art of Negotiation

Analyzing the Conflict

- DEFINE THE PROBLEM. Is it shared or not shared? Who owns it? Take the people out of it and just look at the issue. This is difficult, but if you are invested in blaming the other person or, worse, in winning a point, then you create an obstacle to good communication.

- IS CHANGE POSSIBLE? Be realistic. There are elements of life that one cannot change, but change is possible and, perhaps, desirable in a variety of situations. You or your partner can change how you respond so that you are more comfortable with the outcome of conflicts.

- EXPLORE YOUR OPTIONS. Try to be realistic and creative and to help one another. Just because you raised the problem, it doesn't mean your partner is solely responsible for the resolution.

- FIND A RESOLUTION AND ACT ON IT! It is important not just to accept the problem as a problem, but rather to identify and agree that something is a problem and then make some decisions toward resolution. The decision may be to try one or another resolution and see how it works for an agreed upon amount of time. Very often, couples will agree to a resolution, but never implement it. Don't waste each other's time if you have no intention of working toward the solution. It may not be the perfect solution, but if you have worked it out together and you both feel reasonably good about it, then you owe it to the process to try it.

Defining the Process

- COMPLAINT: An issue that one partner wants to discuss with the other partner.

- REQUEST FOR CHANGE: A specific change that is being requested in the partner's behavior. (Not every interaction will include a bid for change.)

- PRESENTER: The partner making the complaint and/or requesting the change.

- RESPONDER: The partner to whom the request is being made.

Ground Rules and Guidelines

The next time you have a disagreement:

- PLAN AHEAD. Sit down and face one another. Successful negotiations are never accomplished "on the run." If you're never in the same place at the same time, make an appointment to have the conversation over the phone when both parties are able to face the issue fresh, without the distractions of home or work.

- HOLD ONTO YOUR THOUGHTS AND FEELINGS without "acting on them" until you can sit down unencumbered with uninterrupted time. Use the time while you wait to sort out your feelings.

  Sometimes we are responding to other stressors in our lives, or an interaction has pushed our buttons based on old emotions from long-past situations. Often we are projecting our feelings onto our partner when those feelings have more to do with a fight with a friend or a bad interaction with a boss or co-worker.

- ASK FOR WHAT YOU WANT. Share with your partner what changes you feel may need to be made. The purpose of fighting is not always to make a bid for change in the relationship; however, often some kind of change is the outcome that permits both partners to feel resolved about any given issue. Other times, you might simply express your need to be "heard" and "understood" by your partner.

- LISTEN ACTIVELY. Repeat what you think your partner said, and listen as he/she replays for you what you said. A good way to start is by saying, "I think what you are saying is. . . ." Then, "Am I right?"

  If you need clarification of some points, ask with sensitivity. Make sure you do not communicate that your partner is "wrong," but that your emphasis was on something else.

- BE PATIENT. Give your partner the same opportunity to share his/her feelings with you. Repeat this process. It may take some time to become comfortable with this process, and it may even feel awkward. But you will feel "heard" at the end of it.

• RESTATE THE ISSUES. Restate what has been said, and negotiate the appropriate changes or solutions that you feel need to be made. Begin by saying, "The issue appears/seems to be . . . . I have an idea for resolving this issue . . . ."

Exercise 10. Loaded Words or Phrases

Loaded words or phrases push your partner's buttons. They usually communicate judgment and negativity and refer to old, unresolved issues. The following is a short list of loaded words and phrases. Add some of your own.

- "It's all your fault"
- "You did" or "You always" or "You are"
- "You never" or "You shouldn't"

Exercise 11. Repair Attempts

(Reprinted with permission from John M. Gottman and Nan Silver, *The Seven Principles for Making Marriage Work,* copyright 1999 by John M. Gottman, Ph.D. and Nan Silver. By permission of Crown Publishers, a division of Random House, Inc.)

Do this exercise individually, and then share with the group and score with the facilitator.

During our attempts to resolve conflict:

1. We are good at taking breaks when we need them.   _____T _____F

2. My partner usually accepts my apologies.   _____T _____F

3. I can say that I am wrong.   _____T _____F

4. I am pretty good at calming myself down.   _____T _____F

5. We can maintain a sense of humor.   _____T _____F

6. When my partner says we should talk to each other in a
   different way, it usually makes a lot of sense.   _____T _____F

7. My attempts to repair our discussions when they get
   negative are usually effective. _____T _____F

8. We are pretty good listeners when we have different
   positions on things. _____T _____F

9. If things get heated, we can usually pull out of it and
   change things. _____T _____F

10. My partner is good at soothing me when I get upset. _____T _____F

11. I feel confident that we can resolve most issues
    between us. _____T _____F

12. When I comment on how we could communicate better
    my partner listens to me. _____T _____F

13. Even if things get hard at times I know we can get past
    our differences. _____T _____F

14. We can be affectionate even when we disagree. _____T _____F

15. Teasing and humor usually work to get my partner
    over negativity. _____T _____F

16. We can start all over again and improve our discussion
    when we need to. _____T _____F

17. When emotions run hot, expressing how upset I feel
    usually makes a real difference. _____T _____F

18. We can discuss even big differences between us. _____T _____F

19. My partner expresses appreciation for the nice things I do. _____T _____F

20. If I keep trying to communicate it will eventually work. _____T _____F

Exercise 12.   Making Compromises

(Reprinted with permission from John M. Gottman and Nan Silver, *The Seven
Principles for Making Marriage Work*, copyright 1999 by John M. Gottman,

Ph.D. and Nan Silver. By permission of Crown Publishers, a division of Random House, Inc.)

Accepting Influence Questionnaire

Do this exercise individually, and then share with the group and score with the facilitator.

1. I am really interested in my partner's opinions on our basic issues.   _____T _____F

2. I usually learn a lot from my partner even when we disagree.   _____T _____F

3. I want my partner to feel that what he or she says really matters to me.   _____T _____F

4. I generally want my partner to feel influential in this marriage.   _____T _____F

5. I can listen to my partner, but only up to a point.   _____T _____F

6. My partner has a lot of basic common sense.   _____T _____F

7. I try to communicate respect even during our disagreements.   _____T _____F

8. If I keep trying to convince my partner, I will eventually win out.   _____T _____F

9. I don't reject my partner's opinions out of hand.   _____T _____F

10. My partner is not rational enough to take seriously when we discuss our issues.   _____T _____F

11. I believe in lots of give and take in our discussions.   _____T _____F

12. I am very persuasive and usually can win arguments with my partner.   _____T _____F

13. I feel I have an important say when we make decisions.   _____T _____F

14. My partner usually has good ideas.   ____T ____F

15. My partner is basically a great help as a problem solver. ____T ____F

16. I try to listen respectfully, even when we disagree. ____T ____F

17. My ideas for solutions are usually much better than
    my partner's.   ____T ____F

18. I can usually find something to agree with in my
    partner's position.   ____T ____F

19. My partner is usually too emotional.   ____T ____F

20. I am the one who needs to make the big decisions in
    this partnership.   ____T ____F

בָּרוּךְ אַתָּה, יְיָ אֱלֹהֵינוּ, מֶלֶךְ הָעוֹלָם, אֲשֶׁר יָצַר אֶת-הָאָדָם בְּצַלְמוֹ, בְּצֶלֶם דְּמוּת
תַּבְנִיתוֹ, וְהִתְקִין לוֹ מִמֶּנּוּ בִּנְיַן עֲדֵי עַד.
בָּרוּךְ אַתָּה, יְיָ, יוֹצֵר הָאָדָם.

Baruch atah, Adonai Eloheinu, Melech haolam, asher yatzar et haadam
b'tzalmo, b'tzelem d'mut tavnito, v'hitkin lo mimenu binyan adeiad.
Baruch atah Adonai yotzer haadam.

We praise You, *Adonai* our God, Ruler of the universe, Creator of
humankind, a single human fabric woven of love. You have made us in Your
own image, Your own likeness, and we give thanks and praise.
                        Fourth of the Seven Blessings *(Sheva B'rachot)*

At-Home Exercises

Blessing Exercise

Disagreements are inherent in all relationships. Our differences distinguish us
from other human beings. We are blessed in our lives with the ability to tolerate these differences and to be able to learn and grow from others. Create a
blessing for family, friends, and the mutual respect of the differences in the
partnership.

Personal Profiles

Do the following exercise at home individually, and bring it to the next session. This exercise is meant to allow you and your partner to explore the business side of the marriage.

1. What agreements have you made regarding work (i.e., jobs you and your partner have either chosen or agreed upon) for the marriage?

2. Do you like your defined job or role? If not, how would you change it?

3. How have you divided the household chores? Are you happy with your jobs? What would you change?

	Me	My Partner	Not Defined
Purchasing of food?	☐	☐	☐
Cooking?	☐	☐	☐
Maintenance of the house/apartment?	☐	☐	☐
Cleaning the house/apartment?	☐	☐	☐
Laundry/dry cleaning?	☐	☐	☐
Paying bills?	☐	☐	☐
Maintaining the car (if you have one)?	☐	☐	☐
Taking care of the pet (if you have one)?	☐	☐	☐

| Taking the pet to the vet? | ☐ | ☐ | ☐ |
| Making doctor's appointments? | ☐ | ☐ | ☐ |

4. What plans have you made regarding work and career if you have a family?

5. What preferences do you have for a new role or job in the partnership?

6. What does money mean to you?

7. How much time should be devoted to work?

8. How will you distribute money? Will you have joint or separate checking accounts? How much will you save?

9. What have you either learned or been taught about money?

10. Who will be most responsible for maintaining relationships with in-laws and parents vis-à-vis phone calls? Holiday celebrations?

11. How will you share the holidays with family?

Session Five

The Partnership of Marriage

Goals

- To define how a partnership is created

- To explore how each partner views money

- To share histories of families of origin regarding finances

- To look at information regarding your state's laws regarding marital responsibility

- To provide an overview of the fundamental financial and legal changes that will take place after your marriage/union

- To provide basic information on budgeting, bank accounts, managing debt, insurance, savings, investments, and other financial topics

Text Study

There is a great deal of Jewish text not only on money, but on the responsibilities of each partner in a marital relationship.

Isaac married Rebekah, who was a close relative of his father's family, and Jacob, their son, married Leah, then Rachel, his first cousins on his mother's side. From the earliest biblical times, Jews married their close relatives. There were no laws governing whom Jews of that period could and could not marry.

Jacob worked for Laban, his future father-in-law and uncle, seven years in order to marry his beloved Rachel. But Laban tricked Jacob and switched the brides by placing a veil over Leah's face so that Jacob could not make out her features.

Laban wanted his eldest daughter married before the younger one. When Jacob discovered this ruse, he confronted Laban and agreed to work seven more years as a shepherd in order finally to procure the hand of his Rachel (Genesis 29).

Exercise 13. Start-Up Conversation

Ask yourself and your partner these four questions when looking at financial planning and decision making:

1. Are my expectations for my partner and his/her role in the "work" of the relationship realistic?

2. Are my partner's strengths in the areas of my expectations of him/her?

3. Am I expecting my partner to compensate for my limitations?

4. Am I expecting my partner to fill the void of a past failed relationship or a disappointing parental relationship?

Consider This:

You would never consider taking on more job responsibilities if you were dissatisfied with your current position. You might even ask your boss for a change in your job description if you felt that your job was not focusing on your strengths. The same is true for the marital relationship.

If you are a person who is not terribly organized, then you may not be the best partner to pay the bills each month. But maybe you are good with numbers. You and your partner may agree to assign responsibilities for paying the bills. The solution may be for your partner to organize the bills and for you to do the computation and pay the bills. It is important when distributing the "jobs" in the partnership that each of your strengths and limitations is used to its best advantage.

Exercise 14. What Is Your and Your Family's History with Finances?

Do this exercise individually, and then share the answers with the group.

1. **How do you view money and what is your value system regarding it?**

   For example, is money more trouble than it's worth, or is it a necessary evil? Does money bring happiness? Do you need it to feel happy and secure? Will you be fulfilled without it? Is it to be squirreled away? Spent with abandon? Saved for a rainy day? What are your fears and expectations of money?

2. **What is your personal history handling your finances?**

   Do you manage your own finances? Have you lived only with your family, or do you live on your own? Do your parents still support you? Do they plan to continue? When did you first have access to money?

3. **What is your financial situation now?**

   Do you have enough to get by? Is there some discretionary money? Will being married add to the burden or increase the possibilities?

4. **What are your financial plans for the future?**

   Do you have a 401K, an IRA, a life insurance policy? What are your views on these? Do you want to share your information with your partner? When did you first have access to money? What are your fears and expectations of money?

5. **What kind of partnership did your parents have?**

   What were the responsibilities they faced? Did they have parents living with them? Debt? Health issues? Were there other family difficulties that made holding onto money impossible?

   What were their economic backgrounds? Were they similar or different? Did this cause stress in the home or add to the comfort of the family? How did their assumptions and feelings about money affect you? What were the messages you and your siblings received about money?

6. **Is the way you view money influenced by society?**

   What are some of the beliefs your religion holds on money? What about culture? Media? Do you believe there are gender differences in the way you view money? Are men better at managing finances than women?

7. **If you are a same gender couple,** have you discussed how you will manage finances in light of state and local laws regarding property between same sex couples? Are you both comfortable with the decisions you have made?

In a partnership that works for both parties, the following should be true. Together, read and discuss the following traits of a healthy partnership. How many of these traits do you already embody? How can you achieve these traits for yourselves?

- Each partner understands his/her role and has agreed upon the terms of accepting responsibility for that role.

- Each partner understands that the partnership will take effort and agrees to participate in this effort.

- Each partner accepts and understands that the philosophy of "what's in it for me?" does not work in a partnership, but rather is willing to engage in the spirit of giving.

- Each partner feels that the benefits and rewards he/she will reap as a result of his/her efforts will be equitably distributed and will improve the partnership.

- Each partner is committed to the partnership being based on honesty.

- Each partner is willing to be flexible and is ready to reevaluate the partnership when necessary or when one partner makes such a request.

Note: See pages 91–95 for general legal information. This information is reflective of New York State laws, but laws can and do differ significantly from state to state and province to province. If you have specific questions, you should consult your lawyer or your state or provincial government office.

Laws change and circumstances differ; important decisions should be based on the most current and accurate information.

Exercise 15.   Scenario: Emily's Story/Craig's Story

Emily's Story

Emily was one of six children, born right in the middle. Her large family was working class and lived in a modest, low-income housing project with very few amenities, in Brooklyn. Emily's father was employed at the same company for twenty-five years. Emily was in her early teens when he was laid off due to cutbacks within the company.

Emily had to work after school and on the weekends to pay for her clothes and whatever entertainment she had, such as an occasional movie and a soda with friends. She did not have much of a social life in high school, but she was very smart and worked hard. She saved her money and put herself through college.

Emily's mother never complained about their tight living conditions or their inability to provide a better life for their children. She seemed to take it in her stride and never made Emily's father feel responsible for the lack of money in the family. Emily's father took care of the finances and did not share his situation with any member of the family. It was up to Emily's mother to direct the children toward their monetary responsibility to contribute to the family.

When Emily and John met and married, John was already making enough money to support both of them in a very comfortable lifestyle. Emily worked hard, lived modestly, and still managed to save a little. John suggested they pool their money so that they had more for luxuries. Emily was uncomfortable with this. She wanted to control her own money as she had always done. They had never discussed finances prior to their marriage, and John took offense, thinking that she did not trust him.

Discussion Questions

1. How can Emily and John manage to overcome this obstacle?

2. What do you suppose was John's family history regarding money?

3. Is this situation really about trust? If so, how do you encourage trust in the partnership? If not, what is it really about?

4. If you were Emily or John, how would you initiate the first conversation about finances?

5. How often do you think a couple should discuss their financial situation?

Craig's Story

Craig grew up in a well-to-do suburban community. His family seemed to have plenty of discretionary money for vacations, nice clothes, and summer camp for their three children. Craig did not appear to want for anything and went out with a crowd of kids who were from similar backgrounds.

He remembers laying awake some nights listening to his parents argue over money and bills. His mother always referred to living above their means, but he does not remember any of the specifics. Neither Craig's mother nor the children were ever asked to cut back their expenses in any way. They belonged to a country club, drove luxury cars, and had expensive clothes. They maintained their lifestyle by carrying large amounts of debt, which Craig assumed was an acceptable method of managing finances.

When Craig and Deborah decided to get married, they did not discuss their finances. Craig's model had been for the male partner to assume responsibility for finances, and he insisted that he manage the money. Deborah agreed, since this was the same model she had known in her parents' marriage. When Craig suggested they buy an expensive co-op with a large mortgage, Deborah did not ask how they would pay for it, but merely assumed they had sufficient money to cover the cost comfortably. Deborah got an inkling they were in trouble when they got their first delinquent notice for the mortgage.

The next indicator came when the credit card company called to say they were over the limit. Craig had borrowed money against their card to pay the mortgage and had never paid the bill. Deborah was scared and feared they would lose the co-op. She confronted Craig, and he told her not to worry, he was in control of the situation.

Discussion Questions

1. What do you think of this situation as it relates to the building of a partnership?

2. How could Craig and Deborah have prevented this from happening?

3. Was Craig deliberately trying to keep Deborah from understanding their financial situation? Did Craig fully understand their financial situation?

4. Was Craig being irresponsible? How would you feel if your partner was irresponsible?

5. What kind of an impact do you suppose this situation had on their relationship?

6. Discuss how you would communicate to your partner if you felt his/her skills were better suited for a different role in the partnership.

Exercise 16.   Assessment of Skills, Strengths, and Life Experiences

As you review and answer these questions, keep in mind that you are assessing your own and your partner's areas of strengths. You may not be strong in all areas, and neither will your partner, but try to be honest. The purpose of this exercise is to assess the skills you and your partner bring to the relationship as well as areas in which you can support one another.

1. What are the mental strengths of the partnership?
   (areas of competency, practicality, intelligence, talent, interest)

2. What are the physical strengths of the partnership?
   (health, athletic ability, energy level, ability to care for self and others)

3. What are the people skills of the partnership?
   (friendly, poised, good communicator, social, loner, good listener)

4. What are the emotional strengths of the partnership?
   (brave, timid, loving, kind, optimistic, encouraging)

5. What are the life experiences of the partnership?
   (work, relationship, family and travel experiences)

שׁוֹשׂ תָּשִׂישׂ וְתָגֵל צִיּוֹן בְּקִבּוּץ בָּנֶיהָ לְתוֹכָהּ בְּשִׂמְחָה.
בָּרוּךְ אַתָּה, יְיָ, מְשַׂמֵּחַ צִיּוֹן בְּבָנֶיהָ.

Sos tasis v'tageil Tziyon, b'kibutz baneha l'tochah b'simchah. Baruch atah Adonai m'sameiach Tziyon b'vaneha.

You have filled Zion's mouth with song: her children have come back to her in joy! We give thanks to the One who gladdens Zion through her children.

Fifth of the Seven Blessings *(Sheva B'rachot)*

At-Home Exercises

Blessing Exercise

Negotiating a lifestyle between partners is challenging, and one must use creativity to ensure that the needs of each member of the partnership are met.

Create a blessing that describes the ways in which the partnership is rich and acknowledges your gratitude for the creativity between you.

Write a Partnership Agreement

Keeping in mind your assessment of the skills, strengths, and life experiences of your partnership from exercise 16, write an agreement with your partner that includes the following:

1. What do you consider to be discretionary money? How will it be spent?

2. How will you decide on vacations, leisure time?

3. Who will manage discretionary money? Who will pay the bills?

4. What are your priorities as a couple and as individuals?

5. How and where can you comfortably implement your decisions about money?

6. Where do you think you may have to make compromises?

Refer to Rabbi Daniel Judson and Rabbi Nancy Wiener's book, *Meeting at the Well,* chapter 6, for more on finance and picturing your financial future.

Intimacy Profile

Complete the Intimacy Profile below. To prepare for the next session, read "Jewish Attitudes Toward Sexuality and Intimacy" and "Reform Jewish Sexual Values," pages 60–65.

1. List some of the things that give you pleasure.

2. List some of the things that you believe give your partner pleasure.

3. How will you find time for intimacy in your lives?

4. List ways of keeping your love fresh and interesting.

5. Define what intimacy means to you.

6. Is intimacy important to you? If you do not equate sexual intimacy with emotional intimacy, how well are your needs being met in both the sexual and emotional areas of your relationship? Do you and your partner agree on how often you feel the need for sexual contact?

7. Do work and fatigue affect how you feel about being intimate with your partner?

8. Do you use medication that affects your libido? Alcohol? Drugs?

9. Do you believe there are gender differences with regard to the need or desire for intimacy?

10. Does premenstrual syndrome (PMS) affect you or your partner? Does this impact negatively on your sexual relationship? How do you handle it when and if it comes up?

11. Are there other emotional issues that affect your sexual responses? How are you dealing with them?

12. What about environmental factors? Do noise, temperature, interruptions, or other unmentioned factors interfere with your lovemaking and concentration? How do you deal with these?

13. What about the daily stressors of work and scheduling? How will children enter into this equation?

Sexuality and Intimacy

Goals

- To review the biblical and talmudic teachings on intimacy between partners
- To consider the psychosocial factors that impact on sexual intimacy
- To explore human responses to sexuality and intimacy
- To discuss environmental factors that impact on positive sexual relations

Text Study

The following are biblical and talmudic references to marriage that reflect different stages of life and types of relationships and illustrate how having a life partner enhances one's life.

> *Ani l'dodi v'dodi li*—I am my beloved's and my beloved is mine.
>
> Song of Songs 6:3

Many scholars regard the Song of Songs as a collection of lyric love poems. This book offers a description of an ideal relationship, both loving and mutually accepting, in which both lovers initiate sexual intimacy. Both partners' voices are prominent.

> There are three sights which warm my heart and are beautiful in the eyes of the Divine One: concord among peoples, friendship among neighbors, and a man and wife who are inseparable.
>
> Wisdom of Ben Sira 24:1

If the wife you have is small,
Bend to her and whisper all!

> Babylonian Talmud, *Bava M'tzia* 59a

If husband and wife are worthy, the Divine Presence abides with them.

> Babylonian Talmud, *Sotah* 17a

Before a man marries, his love goes to his parents; after he marries, his love goes to his wife.

> *Pirkei D'Rabbi Eliezer* 32a

Two are better than one.

> Ecclesiastes 4:9

Hence, a man leaves his father and mother and clings to his wife, so that they become one flesh.

> Genesis 2:24

A man who does not have a wife lives without joy, without blessing, and without goodness. In the West they said: "Without Torah and without moral protection." Rabbi ben Ulla said: "And without peace."

> Babylonian Talmud, *Y'vamot* 63b

Where there is no union of male and female, men are not worthy of beholding the *Shechinah* [Divine Presence].

> *Zohar,* vol. 3, *Acharei Mot,* p. 50a

Jewish Attitudes Toward Sexuality and Intimacy

(From the Ad Hoc Committee on Human Sexuality Report to the CCAR 1998)

As liberal Jews, we seek to understand human sexuality and sexual expression in a religious context. While we are aware that at this point in our history the value systems of many liberal Jews are based upon contemporary secular norms, it is our belief that Reform Judaism can speak meaningfully to all aspects of our lives, including intimate human relationships. In framing a religious value system that can guide all of us in making decisions about our sexuality we utilize religious principles derived from our Reform predecessors. These principles are based upon the threefold approach which Reform Judaism has developed in the course of its history: universalism, particularism, and contemporary knowledge. This threefold approach can be expressed through the following guiding principles:

1. **B'riah** (The Created Universe): We exist as part of a vast and varied world fashioned by a purposeful Creator. "When God created humanity, God made Adam in the Divine image . . . male and female . . . and God found it very good" (Genesis 1:27–31). Creator and creature are bound together through this intentional act. B'riah reminds us that our human uniqueness and diversity, including our sexuality, are ultimately derived from the conscious Divine act of creation and as such are purposeful and positive.

2. **Am B'rit** (People of the Covenant): As Jews we also exist as part of a particular people which has a unique and holy relationship with God. After entering into covenant with God at Sinai, our people responded by saying, "All the Eternal God has spoken we will faithfully do" (Exodus 24:7). Each generation, like the first one at Sinai, is committed to responsible action, the essential confirmation of belief. We share a special mandate to preserve this relationship through the Jewish generations of history. We weigh the many voices of our tradition as we seek to find ways for modern Jews to express themselves as sexual beings in an authentically Jewish manner.

3. **Daat** (Contemporary Knowledge): Yosef Albo, a noted medieval Jewish philosopher wrote, "It is impossible that the law of God . . . shall be complete, so that it will be adequate for all times, because the novel conditions that constantly arise in the affairs of men, in laws and in deeds, are too numerous to count" *(Sefer Halkarim,* discourse #3, chapter 23). We draw upon secular knowledge as we engage in holy endeavors. In an age of rapidly expanding information and understanding, to grasp fully human sexuality and its expressions, we believe it is necessary to gain insight and guidance from contemporary knowledge in related fields.

Reform Jewish Sexual Values

Jewish religious values are based upon the unity of God and the integrity of the world and its inhabitants as Divine creations. These values identify *sh'leimut* as a fundamental goal of human experience. The Hebrew root *ShLM* expresses the ideal of wholeness, completeness, unity, and peace.

Sexuality and sexual expression are integral and powerful elements in the potential wholeness of human beings. Our tradition commands us to sanctify the basic elements of the human being through values that express the Divine in every person and in every relationship. Each Jew should seek to conduct his/her sexual life in a manner that elicits the intrinsic holiness within the person and the relationship. Thus can *sh'leimut* be realized. The specific values that follow are contemporary interpretations of human *sh'leimut*:

1. **B'tzelem Elohim** ("in the image of God"). This fundamental Jewish idea, articulated in Genesis 1:27, "And God created Adam in the Divine image . . . male and female . . ." is at the core of all Jewish values. *B'tzelem Elohim* underscores the inherent dignity of every person, woman and man, with equal honor and respect due to each individual's integrity and sexual identity. *B'tzelem Elohim* requires each of us to value one's self and one's sexual partner and to be sensitive to his/her needs. Thus, we do affirm that consensuality and mutuality are among the values necessary to validate a sexual relationship as spiritual and ethical and therefore "in the image of God."

2. **Emet** ("truth"). Authentic and ethical human relationships should be grounded in both truth and honesty. "These are the things you are to do: speak the truth to one another, render true and perfect justice in your gates" (Zechariah 8:16). People can only truly know each other and appreciate the Divine in all people when they come to each other openly and honestly. Both partners in an intimate relationship should strive to communicate lovingly. They should tell each other what gives them sexual pleasure and what does not, and should honestly share their love as well as the challenges that their relationship presents to them. However, honesty which is destructive of the relationship lacks the quality of *rachamim*, mercy. "Mercy and truth shall meet, justice and peace shall embrace" (Psalm 85:11). For that reason, intimate partners should be mindful that there may be moments when they are better served by not being totally candid with each other. In addition, falsehood which manipulates is sinful. Dating partners must not lie to each other in order to mislead the other into a sexual relationship. Neither partner should use the other as a sexual object. Finally, parents should learn how to teach their children both the facts and the consequences of sexual behavior, physically, emotionally, and spiritually. Parents should then use that teaching to help their children face the realities of their contemporary world.

3. **B'ri-ut** ("health"). Our tradition enjoins upon us the responsibility to rejoice in and to maximize our physical, emotional, and spiritual health. "Blessed is our Eternal God, Creator of the universe, who has made our bodies with wisdom, combining veins, arteries, and vital organs into a finely balanced network" (*Gates of Prayer* [1975], page 284). Reform Judaism encourages adults of all ages and physical and mental capabilities to develop expressions of their sexuality that are both responsible and joyful. The abuse of human sexuality can be destructive to our emotional, spiritual, and physical health.

We have a duty to engage only in those sexual behaviors that do not put others or ourselves at risk. In our age of HIV/AIDS and epidemic sexually transmitted diseases, irresponsible sexual behavior can put our lives and the lives of others at risk. We must act with the knowledge that our sexual behavior is linked to our physical health.

4. **Mishpat** ("justice"). Judaism enjoins upon us the mandate to reach out and care for others, to treat all of those created in the image of God with respect and dignity, to strive to create equality and justice wherever people are treated unfairly, to help meet the needs of the less fortunate, and to engage in *tikkun olam,* the repair of God's creation. The prophet Amos exhorts us to "let justice well up as waters, righteousness as a mighty stream" (Amos 5:24). As a people who have historically suffered at the hands of the powerful, we must be especially sensitive to any abuse of power and victimization of other human beings. According to the Sages, the *yetzer hara,* through its sexual component, may sometimes lead to destructive behavior and to sin. All forms of sexual harassment, incest, child molestation, and rape violate the value of *mishpat.* Our pursuit of *mishpat* should inspire us to eradicate prejudice, inequality, and discrimination based upon gender or sexual orientation.

5. **Mishpachah** ("family"). The family is a cornerstone of Jewish life. The Torah, through the first mitzvah, *p'ru ur'vu,* "be fruitful and multiply" (Genesis 1:28), emphasizes the obligation of bringing children into the world through the institution of the family. In our age, the traditional notion of family as being two parents and children (and perhaps older generations) living in the same household is in the process of being redefined. Men and women of various ages living together, singles, gay and lesbian couples, and single-parent households, etc., may all be understood as families in the wider, if not traditional, sense. "Family" also has multiple meanings in an age of increasingly complex biotechnology and choice. While procreation and family are especially important as guarantors of the survival of the Jewish people, all Jews have a responsibility to raise and nurture the next generation of our people. The importance of family, whether biological or relationally based, remains the foundation of meaningful human existence.

6. **Tz'niut** ("modesty"). The classic *Iggeret HaKodesh,* "The Holy Letter," sets forth the Jewish view that the Holy One did not create anything that is not beautiful and potentially good. The human body in itself is never to be considered an object of shame or embarrassment. Instead, ". . . it is the manner and context in which it [i.e., the body] is utilized, the ends to which it is used, which determine condemnation or praise." Our behavior should never reduce the human body to being an object. Dress, language, and behavior should reflect a sensitivity to the Jewish respect for modesty and privacy. As Jews we acknowl-

edge and celebrate the differences between public, private, and holy time as well as the differences between public, private, and holy places.

7. **B'rit** ("covenantal relationship"). For sexual expression in human relationships to reach the fullness of its potential, it should be grounded in fidelity and the intention of permanence. This grounding mirrors the historic Jewish ideal of the relationship between God and the people Israel, with its mutual responsibilities and its assumption of constancy. The prophet Hosea wrote, "I will betroth you to Me forever; I will betroth you to Me in righteousness and justice, in love and compassion, I will betroth you to Me in everlasting faithfulness" (Hosea 2:21–22). A sexual relationship is covenantal when it is stable and enduring and includes mutual esteem, trust, and faithfulness.

8. **Simcha** ("joy"). Human sexuality, as a powerful force in our lives, has the potential for physical closeness and pleasure, emotional intimacy and communication. The experience of sexual pleasure and orgasm, both in relationships and individually, can greatly delight women and men. Our tradition teaches that procreation is not the sole purpose of sexual intimacy; it not only recognizes but also rejoices in the gratification which our sexuality can bring to us. As an expression of love, the physical release and relaxation, the enjoyment of sensuality and playfulness, which responsible sexual activity can provide is encouraged by our Jewish tradition. The Sages teach that the *Shechinah,* the Divine Presence, joins with people when they unite in love, but add that if there is no joy between them, the *Shechinah* will not be present (*Shabbat* 30b, *Zohar* l). Judaism insists that the *simchah* of human sexual activity should be experienced only in healthy and responsible human relationships.

9. **Ahavah** ("love"). The mitzvah from Leviticus 19:18, "You shall love your neighbor as yourself; I am *Adonai,*" serves as an essential maxim of all human relationships. The same Hebrew value term, *ahavah,* is used to describe the ideal relationship between God and humanity as well as between people. The Jewish marriage ceremony speaks of *ahavah v'achavah, shalom v'rei-ut,* "love and affection, wholeness and friendship" as ideals which should undergird holy relationships. For Jews *ahavah* is not only a feeling or emotion, but also the concrete behaviors we display toward God and our fellow humans. *Ahavah* implies "self-esteem," the internal conviction that each of us should appear worthy in our own eyes. To be loved, one must consider oneself lovable; without regard for self, one can hardly care for others. *Ahavah* forbids any abuse or violence in sexual or any aspect of human relationships. *Ahavah* should be expressed through behavior which displays caring, support, and empathy.

10. **K'dushah** ("holiness"). This value comes from the root meaning of the Hebrew word *KDSh,* "distinct from all others, unique, set apart for an elevated purpose." The Torah instructs us: "You shall be holy, for I, *Adonai* your God, am holy" (Leviticus 19:2). Holiness is not simply a state of being; rather it is a continuing process of human striving for increasingly higher levels of moral living. In a Reform Jewish context, a relationship may attain a measure of *k'dushah* when both partners voluntarily set themselves apart exclusively for each other, thereby finding unique emotional, sexual, and spiritual intimacy.

Self-esteem is tied to a positive body image. Again, Judaism diverges from other faiths in that Judaism teaches that both the body and the spirit are God's creation, both are holy, worthy of praise and positive feelings. In order for couples to find sexual pleasure and satisfaction, they must both have a positive body image. This does not necessarily mean they must have "perfect" bodies, as in the image put forth by magazines and supermodels. People of all body types and those with physical disabilities are all seen as special and, indeed, holy.

Therefore, the care of one's body is critical to the enjoyment of sexual activity between partners. Because we are created in the divine image, and our bodies are ours only for temporary use on this earth, we must care for our bodies in a dignified and sensitive way. There is an expression: "cleanliness is akin to holiness." For sexual pleasure and satisfaction, cleanliness is clearly a prerequisite.

Other Influences on Your Sexual Life

State of Mind

You are what you feel, and your responses and your ability to take pleasure in your sexual encounters with your partner are deeply affected by your state of mind. Negativity has a great impact on how receptive you are to intimacy. Negativity can prevent sexual arousal and other physical responses that would encourage your partner in pursuing more contact.

Fear, anger, grief, contempt, and frustration can affect a successful sexual encounter. While some individuals find these emotions have intensified their sexual experiences, generally they have a negative impact. One of the sages of our religion, Maimonides, taught that one may not have sexual intercourse "while in mourning . . . or if a husband and wife quarreled during the daytime and have not resolved it by nightfall." The famous saying "Never go to bed angry" is also attributed to Maimonides.

State of Body

Your physical and mental state is important not only to the frequency of your sexual intimacy, but to the quality. Too often, individuals don't see their doctors when there is something not quite right with the way they are feeling physically. Taking time from work and busy schedules makes visiting a doctor difficult, so we tend to go only when there is an absolute necessity. Don't wait for a crisis situation. Your physical well-being is important to your partner on many levels, including your sexual life together.

Our fast-paced society also has an impact on your feelings of sexuality. Stress will affect your interest in lovemaking and needs to be addressed within the context of the relationship. Are you just too exhausted to be romantically inclined? Working too hard and too long, lack of sleep, or loss of concentration will doubtlessly affect sexual responses.

To counterbalance the effects of your daily stressors, take time out, even if once a week, to reconnect. Make a date, if you must, for playful, intimate time together. The goal need not be to have sexual intercourse, but merely to enjoy physical contact together. Cuddling, touching, and caressing are good beginnings to feeling warm and physically connected. Let the rest follow on its own.

Medication, Recreational Drugs, and Alcohol

Certain prescription medications, such as cold tablets, antihistamines, blood pressure medication, and drugs taken for anxiety, depression, and other psychological disorders, can affect not only the sex drive, but sexual response. It is important to ask your physician about the side effects of any long-term drugs you may be taking and to discuss this honestly with your partner. Then you can develop a strategy for dealing with the situation together.

Recreational drugs affect your sexual responses. Frequently, drug users don't notice differences in their sexual activities between using or not using drugs. However, most drugs diminish the need or desire for sexual intimacy. Most street drugs are depressants. They will not enhance your lovemaking, but will more likely impact negatively on having good sex.

Similarly, alcohol is a depressant. A few glasses of wine or several alcoholic drinks may temporarily make you the "life of the party," but then you will notice a sharp drop, your senses and your reflexes will dull, and sleepiness will usually follow. In short, alcohol is not a turn-on.

Clearly, it is not desirable or advisable for you to use recreational stimulants or depressants. They negatively affect your health, mental well-being, and your ability to function as a sexual partner. If you are currently using recreational drugs, it is advisable either to stop on your own or to get some assistance in this area.

Premenstrual Syndrome

Not every woman suffers from the effects of premenstrual syndrome (PMS), but PMS has recently become part of the medical lexicon, referring to a medical condition that is best described as a hormonal (part of the endocrine system) fluctuation that has possible psychological components. Many men and women, having grown up with negative connotations associated with PMS and the stereotypes associated with this disorder, have now come to understand and, hopefully, empathize with their partners and loved ones who suffer from PMS.

It is important for women to become attuned to their biorhythms, learning to calculate if and when they experience the onset of PMS and what impact it has on their physical and emotional being. Many women report extreme personality changes, including moodiness, irritability, or depression. There are physical components, such as feelings of being swollen, bloated, and engorged, that add to the discomfort experienced by almost a third of women who have PMS.

If you think you may suffer from PMS, you should discuss this with your physician; there are medications that can alleviate the side effects of this syndrome. It is advisable also to discuss this with your partner so that what may appear to be random mood swings are not misinterpreted and are understood to be part of a physical condition.

Environmental Factors

Is there a dog barking, a baby crying, a television playing, or loud music? Is it too hot, too cold, thundering, or lightning? Sometimes noises and other nuisances become distractions that we just cannot overcome. The mood is either lost or cannot be attained, but don't try to force it. Sometimes, you must agree to try again under better circumstances. Try not to take this personally. These outside factors affect everyone.

Fear of Pregnancy

For many couples, fear of pregnancy is an obstacle that they have to work hard to overcome. The need to stop the process of lovemaking to use contraceptives can be somewhat inhibiting. This is a good time to remember your sense of humor and your love for one another. Discuss your birth control options, and agree on a method that makes both of you comfortable.

Performance Anxiety

Performance anxiety is more prevalent than one would imagine. What is performance anxiety? It is not dissimilar from stage fright. Fear and anxiety prevent individuals from performing as they would normally. Performance anxiety may manifest itself in somatizing (the manufacturing of ailments) or by the physical inability to perform sexually. This is not unusual for newly married couples, who are eager to please. It is most often cured by relaxation techniques and other similar interventions. The best thing to do is to not worry and to be supportive of your partner.

Erectile Dysfunction (ED)

Erectile Dysfunction (ED) is a condition that affects many men at some point in their lives. It is characterized as the inability to achieve or maintain an erection for a duration sufficient to satisfy his or his partner's needs.

The term "erectile dysfunction" is used to describe a variety of occurrences, such as the inability to achieve erection, an inconsistent ability to do so, or the ability to achieve erection for a brief amount of time. These diverse definitions make it difficult to ascertain the actual incidence of "erectile dysfunction." Incidence does mostly correlate to age, with the larger percentage of occurrence in men between the ages of 40 and 65. Sporadic, or transient ED affects as much as 50% of the male population between the ages of 40 and 70, though it can, and does, affect much younger men as well, to a lesser degree.

Often, ED is linked to the onset of certain diseases, such as

- diabetes,
- kidney disease,
- alcoholism and drug abuse;
- neurological conditions, and
- vascular disorders

which account for as many as 70% of the cases of chronic ED.

Psychological factors, such as

- stress
- anxiety and
- depression

may account for as many as 20% of the cases.

Frequent ED can create, even in its transient form, some emotional unrest and a lessening of self-esteem. For many couples this is a painful experience and they avoid direct confrontation of the problem. Unfortunately, avoidance does not permit either party to achieve any degree of comfort, either from the support they may receive or from the reassurance that it is not an outgrowth of any changes in their feelings for one another. On the other hand, having an open and honest dialogue will significantly relieve the tension that may be building as a result of the disruption to regular intimacy. If you find, at any time in the relationship, that ED does occur and you are not confronting the issue, this may signal a need for intervention by a professional. A visit to your family doctor should necessarily be the first step in order to rule out any physiological problems. Once you have been reassured it is not of a physical nature, it may be appropriate to speak with a mental health professional. Treatment and intervention, along with medications, where it is deemed necessary, are highly successful.

Communication

Communication is the key to a good sexual relationship. Communication that is loving, trusting, and open will engender warmth, sensitivity, and loving responses, generating a mutually rewarding sexual relationship. It is worth working at and will keep you both satisfied within the context of the marriage.

Expectations

A person's expectations can profoundly impact a couple's sexual relationship. What are your expectations for your sexual relationship together? Have you thought about where these expectations come from and how they have affected the way you have conducted your intimate life? What are your views on marital fidelity? Do you accept infidelity as inevitable in today's society, or are you committed to keeping your marital vows sacred?

According to theologian/psychologist Andrew M. Greeley, marital fidelity means more than "staying out of someone else's bed." Fidelity means "creating an irresistible lover out of a very human partner," says Greeley. "In lovemaking, you get what you earn." Making your partner feel irresistible will be an enormous turn-on and will result in increased sexual responsiveness.

Exercise 17.   Our Sexual Relationship

1. My partner and I discuss our sexual relationship openly
   and honestly.   ____T ____F

2. My partner and I are very open about our
   sexual problems.   ____T ____F

3. I am too embarrassed to let my partner know my
   likes and dislikes.   ____T ____F

4. I am frequently too stressed to think about our
   sexual relationship.   ____T ____F

5. I feel disappointed by our sexual relationship
   at times.   ____T ____F

6. I would like to have more time for intimacy in
   our relationship.   ____T ____F

7. We never seem to make enough time for sexual
   intimacy.   ____T ____F

8. We don't talk about our sexual disagreements.   ____T ____F

9. I almost never share my expectations for our
   sexual relationship.   ____T ____F

10. Fidelity is something I take for granted, but we don't
    talk about it.   ____T ____F

11. I am easily distracted, but I never mention this.   ____T ____F

שַׂמֵּחַ תְּשַׂמַּח רֵעִים הָאֲהוּבִים כְּשַׂמֵּחֲךָ יְצִירְךָ בְּגַן עֵדֶן מִקֶּדֶם. בָּרוּךְ אַתָּה, יְיָ,
מְשַׂמֵּחַ חָתָן וְכַלָּה.

*Samei-ach t'samach rei-im haahuvim k'sameichacha y'tzircha b'Gan Eden
mikedem. Baruch atah, Adonai, m'samei-ach chatan v'chalah.*

May these loving companions rejoice as have Your creatures since the days
of Creation. We praise You, *Adonai* our God, who causes bride and groom
to rejoice.

Sixth of the Seven Blessings *(Sheva B'rachot)*

At-Home Exercises

Blessing Exercise

We have all experienced different family models. Some may feel more or less blessed, but we have learned from our past. Create a blessing that shares how you feel about the physical and emotional intimacy that has been brought into your life.

Jewish Messages from Your Family

This exercise is to be done at home. Answer the questions alone, and then share them.

Please refer to your companion book, *Meeting at the Well*, chapter 7, "Religion: Asking Life's Big Jewish Questions." If you are of another faith, answer these questions reflecting your family's viewpoint and practices on days of religious observance.

1. Was marrying someone Jewish important to your parents?

2. What was the message from your family of origin regarding intermarriage? Differences? How did you interpret those messages?

3. Would you describe your family as spiritual? If yes, how? If no, does this impact on your own need for spirituality?

4. Was being Jewish important to your family of origin? How did they express this importance?

5. Did your family make giving *tzedakah* (charity) a priority? As a child, were you involved in decisions about *tzedakah*? Were the choices for *tzedakah* Jewish choices?

6. Did your family do community service with a Jewish outlook?

7. Did your family engage in political activism with a Jewish outlook?

8. Did you belong to a synagogue?

9. Did you go to synagogue on the High Holy Days?

10. Did you go to synagogue on Shabbat?

11. Did you light Shabbat candles?

12. Did you have a family Shabbat dinner?

13. Did you celebrate Chanukah? Light candles in a menorah?

14. Did you have a Passover seder? Did you further observe Passover by (a) ridding the house of *chameitz,* (b) eating matzah for the duration of the festival, (c) reading the *Haggadah*?

15. Did you celebrate Shavuot? Tishah B'Av? Sukkot? Simchat Torah? Tu BiSh'vat?

16. Did you go to religious school? Did you become a bar or bat mitzvah? Were you confirmed?

17. Did you go to Hebrew day school?

18. Did you go to Jewish summer camp?

19. Were you a member of a Jewish youth group?

20. Did you visit Israel?

21. Did you listen to Jewish and/or Israeli music?

22. Was Israel important in your family?

23. Do you have any family members who made *aliyah*? How did your family feel about this? Have you ever thought about making *aliyah*?

24. Was your first date Jewish?

25. Did you ever date someone who was not Jewish?

26. Was it important to go to a college with a significant Jewish population? Did you join Hillel? A Jewish fraternity or sorority? Jewish social action organizations? Zionist organizations?

Your Jewish Identity

1. What does being Jewish mean to you?

2. How important is Jewish tradition in your life?

3. What parts of Jewish tradition are meaningful to you today? Why?

4. Do you identify your Jewish identity in cultural, historical, ethnic, and/or religious terms?

5. How important is your Jewish identity to you?

6. How do you see Judaism reflected in your daily life? In your life choices? In your understanding of the world? In your values?

If You Are of Another Faith

1. What does your birth religion mean to you?

2. How does your family respond to the idea of your having a Jewish home?

3. What are your plans for including your family in holiday celebrations?

4. How important was religion in your family of origin?

5. Did you enjoy rituals and traditions surrounding your birth religion?

6. How did your birth religion impact on your values?

7. Was religion a part of your social life as you were growing up?

8. How do you plan to be part of your family's holiday celebrations?

If You Do Not Identify with Being Jewish at This Time in Your Life

1. Was there some defining moment and/or act that distanced you from Judaism?

2. Do you feel you were influenced by choices made by family members?

3. Are you and your partner similarly identified?

4. How will your similarities and/or differences be reflected in your decisions for your home?

Basic Information about Jewish Weddings

The Jewish wedding ceremony is rich in symbolism. Every aspect of Jewish culture is incorporated into and expressed in this beautiful ritual. In the Jewish viewpoint, this is fitting because marriage is a religious observance, an emotional commitment, a business arrangement, and an artistic expression, replete with ancient customs and superstitions. Marriage is the bringing together of two people, two families, two separate streams of history and culture and making them one.

There are three essential symbols that grew from the legal core of what constitutes a Jewish marriage—the *chuppah*, the *ketubah*, and the ring. The home is represented by the central symbol of the Jewish wedding, the *chuppah*, the canopy under which the couple are joined in marriage. The *chuppah* can be a personal expression for each couple, such as the use of a *tallit* to cover the couple. The *tallit* may have some symbolic significance to either the bride or the groom. The *chuppah* may be something created especially for the occasion by a member of the bride's or groom's family, or by family or friends, or it may be a canopy made from flowers and fabric. Under the *chuppah*, you are entering and creating your own sacred space together as a new family.

The *ketubah* is a covenant between two partners. Though the language may differ from text to text and the design may vary from simple to more elaborate, this covenant mirrors the covenant made between God and the Children of Israel at Mount Sinai.

In ancient times, this document outlined the dowry, usually represented by monies and goods, which a bride would bring to a marriage. As well, it stipulated what the woman would take away from the marriage should it be dissolved by death or divorce. For many couples today, the *ketubah* has become less a legal document and more a symbolic commitment to their marital responsibilities and egalitarian relationship.

The symbolic gesture of exchanging rings makes the couple's commitment binding. In prior times, this was achieved by the giving of coins, but long ago the ring, symbolizing eternity, replaced this.

A vow of consecration accompanies the sacred exchange of simple gold rings. The ceremony is concluded by the recitation of the Seven Blessings *(Sheva B'rachot)*, usually by the officiating representative of the Jewish faith, but it may be recited by a friend or family member. These seven blessings link your wedding with the creation of humankind, to Creation itself, and to your larger Jewish family, the Jewish people.

For centuries, it was the tradition to have seven nights of dinners and festivities following the wedding ceremony. The Seven Blessings were, and in some communities still are, recited at each of these festive meals. The purpose of these dinners is to entertain the couple, helping them to feel part of the larger community and to make the transition into married life.

In some traditional communities, friends and relatives take responsibility for keeping the couple's minds off sexual relations, as their consummation necessarily prohibits cohabitation for about two weeks after their first encounter. This is not the custom in the Reform Jewish community. In the large majority of communities, the honeymoon has replaced these festivities.

The language of the Seven Blessings emphasizes the source of blessings in every aspect of life. It is these blessings that have been reaffirmed at the end of each session. This is a time to reflect on all your blessings and to be reminded of the source of our blessings.

Our Jewish Home

Goals

- To explore how Judaism can enrich your life and partnership

- To define your expectations for the role of Judaism in your marriage

- To discuss decisions about children and related genetic issues

- To learn how to mediate differences in Jewish practices within your home

- To examine the importance of holiday celebrations for you and your partner

This session will be co-led by the facilitator and a rabbi. The rabbi will address the issues above and will also bring information and a particular perspective to the group on the creation of a Jewish home. Please be prepared to review some of the information in your previous week's at-home exercise.

There are many beautiful rituals that may be incorporated into your engagement ceremonies/parties into which you may wish to delve more deeply. We hope you will consult with your rabbi during this process to find out how you can make this unique time in your lives richer and more meaningful.

Our tradition is rich in symbolism, and we will share with you some of the beauty of our customs and their rich history as we discuss your wedding and what it means to create a sacred space for you and your loved ones.

Text Study

It was the custom when a boy was born to plant a cedar tree; and when a girl was born, an acacia tree. When they married, the trees were cut down and the wedding canopy was woven from their branches.

Babylonian Talmud, *Gittin* 57a

The Wedding Ceremony

What is a *chuppah,* and where did it come from?

The *chuppah* is the canopy under which a couple stands. The Bible indicates that the *chuppah* was a tent or room belonging to the bridegroom: "the bridegroom coming forth from his *chuppah*" (Psalm 19:6); "Let the bridegroom come forth from his chamber and the bride from her *chuppah*" (Joel 2:16). It is believed that the groom's father, in honor of his son's marriage, often built this *chuppah*, or marriage room. The Midrash and the Talmud offer many references of such loving generosity by the groom's father in building a decorative *chuppah* for his son.

The custom of having a wedding canopy hang above the bride and groom arose around the sixteenth century, and though it had the air of an ancient custom, it was somewhat difficult to find the source of its development. Some scholars have interpreted the word *chuppah* to signify the retiring of the bride and groom to a place of privacy. Others explained it as the actual bringing of the bride to the groom's house for the purpose of marriage. Others speculate that *chuppah* means "the spreading of the cloth *[tallit]* over the head" during the reciting of the blessing.

In twelfth-century France, the *chuppah* referred to the covering of the bride's and groom's heads with a colored cloth during the ceremony. In Germany in the thirteenth and fourteenth centuries, the custom was to provide a pavilion, called a *chuppah*, in which the bride and the groom sat together.

The *chuppah* has developed into a primary symbol in a Jewish wedding ceremony. Whether the *chuppah* is a structure or a canopy, the Jewish home is seen as having its beginning as the couple consecrates each other through their vows. The *chuppah* arching over the couple becomes a blanket of protection, a source of comfort, and symbolically represents the creation of a new Jewish home.

When you think about the implications of what that means, the *chuppah*'s power as a symbol becomes clearer. A Jewish home is not just a place where Jews reside; rather it is a haven, a refuge, and at times, a shelter from the storm. It is a place from which individuals, couples, and families gather strength, share their intimate moments, and partake in the rituals and traditions of their heritage that bind them to one another, linking them from generation to generation *(l'dor v'dor)*. It is a place where values and morals are shared, imparted, and practiced. The Jewish home is more than a house, because the individuals who enrich their surroundings make it more than a mere protection from the elements.

What is a *ketubah*?

The earliest known Jewish marriage contract dating from about 440 B.C.E. was discovered amongst a collection of Aramaic papyri at Assuan and Elephantine, Egypt, in 1905. The contract comes from the period following the Babylonian capture of Jerusalem, when many Jews emigrated to Egypt and established a Jewish colony there. The details of the marriage settlement are laid forth, along with all the stipulations should one or both of the partners die, or should a divorce ensue. It is clear that the purpose of this document is as much to protect the rights of the woman as the investment of the groom and his family.

Traditionally, a *ketubah* was a document that gave security to the less protected partner, the woman. Because in ancient and medieval times the woman was the more vulnerable partner in marital arrangements, a document was created to provide the woman some solace and comfort. Though protection was limited, it offered a modicum of equality to the woman. The *ketubah* also stipulated the obligations of a wife to a husband, including sexual relations.

Now, there are many versions of the *ketubah,* and the one that is recognized most often within the Reform Movement is more egalitarian. The Conservative Movement's *ketubah* has what is known as the Lieberman Clause, which is essentially a prenuptial agreement that facilitates receiving a *get* (a Jewish divorce). In Liberal Judaism, a *ketubah* can be a beautiful document that shares the mutuality of the relationship and is reflective of tradition.

Where did the custom of exchanging wedding rings come from?

Did you know that in the Middle Ages engagement rings were worn by men rather than by women? In Germany, the bride's father would present the bridegroom with a gold ring prior to the wedding, while the bride did not receive her engagement ring until the morning of her wedding. The Greco-Turkish custom was to give ceremonially an engagement ring to the Jewish maiden immediately. Some of the elders of the congregation, along with a crowd of spectators, visited the future bride and bestowed the ring upon her.

In Italy, the wearing of rings was for the pleasure of both the bride and the bride-groom, to the point that a local ordinance had to be established that read: "No man shall wear more than one gold ring, which he may place on any finger of either hand. No woman shall put on more than two rings on the same occasion, or at the utmost she may wear three rings." The rings were for ordinary use but were clearly overused.

Other customs included the giving of betrothal rings. These were not meant to be worn, as they were very large, with the large hoops ending not with an ordinary bezel, but with elaborate artistic designs in gold, often representing turreted buildings with movable weathercocks at the apex. Some of these are believed to be from the thirteenth century, and most bear the Hebrew inscription *Mazal tov,* "Good luck!"

The wedding rings from this period were unadorned and free of jewels. A gemmed ring could not lawfully be used at a wedding ceremony, as a specialist would be needed to attest to its authenticity and value because it was part of a legal and financial transaction. This was done to protect the bride. At a Jewish wedding ceremony, the ring replaced the exchange of a gift of money or an article of value, which was itself a symbolic survival of the oldest custom of acquiring a bride by direct purchase. The wedding ring is not mentioned in the Talmud, nor was it introduced into the Jewish ceremony until the seventh or eighth century. In its earliest inception, it need not be made of gold—it could be of silver-gilt or even brazen—but there could be no deception; the bride must be informed of what metal it was composed.

Where did the Jewish wedding as a celebration come from?

It is a mitzvah to rejoice with the bride and groom. In the Middle Ages, mostly in Eastern European communities, merrymakers at Jewish weddings had a prominent place. There were already ghettos established for the Jews, and along with social changes in the ghettos, the character and activities of the merrymakers changed. The merrymaker, whether a jester *(leitz), marshellik,* or buffoon *(bad-chan),* had but one task: to amuse the guests at the wedding and to increase the merriment. Merrymakers were not always in favor with the religious leaders of the communities, as they often resorted to less than refined means of merrymaking, but they were so popular with the people that they remained in existence for many generations to come.

By the seventeenth century, a pious asceticism spread across Eastern Europe with a flowering of moralistic Yiddish literature. This was related to the pogroms and the general misfortunes of the Jews, who were led to believe that their woes were the result of having sinned excessively and not being pious enough. It was a period of national depression for the Jews, and merrymaking would have been out of place as Jews searched for the root of their sin. The Council of 1650 issued an edict ordering "that no music should be heard in a Jewish home, except on the night of a wedding."

However, the communities continued to protect and care for their merrymakers, retaining them at festivals and, particularly, weddings. Eastern European weddings were celebrations for the family and its larger Jewish community. It was an opportunity to forget temporarily the burdens and woes of their drab existence and to enter into a joyous occasion of gaiety, music, and dancing. The rabbi and cantor were in command only of the more serious aspects of the wedding ceremony. Later in the Middle Ages, the merrymaker combined the functions of musician and comedian, the Jewish equivalent of the court jester.

By the fifteenth century, various ordinances were being issued describing in great detail appropriate clothing for individuals for occasions, the amount and type of food that might be served, and even the number of guests and musicians who might be invited to these functions. Why was all this necessary?

These ordinances come from the fear that Jews were creating the envy of suspicious gentile neighbors who were aroused by a display of costly garments or jewelry and feasting. An attempt to keep up with the neighbors often led to the impoverishment of families, turning festive celebrations into sorrowful aftermaths. One of the earliest law books of German Jewry shows that expensive festivities at weddings had become customary. These extravagances increased until some communities, such as Constantinople, issued an edict in 1725 restricting even the wealthiest members of the community to a maximum dowry of 1,000 piasters, and wedding gifts to a maximum of one-fifth the value of the dowry.

By the nineteenth century, the customs connected with a Jewish wedding had become so numerous and complex that a specialist was required to assure that all the traditional requirements, religious prescriptions, and local customs were carried out scrupulously. A successful wedding had to be managed down to the last detail by a professional who meticulously observed the correct order of the wedding, from ceremony to celebration. Sounds a bit like a modern-day wedding planner, doesn't it?

We see from these organized communal responses that wedding festivities had begun to get out of hand, requiring the community leaders to limit the excesses that were becoming a measure and means of separating the "haves" and "have-nots." Today, we see many communities and synagogues issuing restrictions on celebrations, such as *b'nei mitzvah,* in an attempt to focus on the true meaning of the religious rite of passage.

What is an *aufruf?*

It is customary for the groom, on the Shabbat prior to the wedding, to receive an *aliyah* at the synagogue. In some communities, after he recites the blessing for reading from the Torah, congregants throw candy or nuts and raisins at him. The ritual, called an *aufruf,* means "going up to the Torah." In some liberal congregations, the bride and groom are called up to the *bimah* to read the blessing and are blessed by the rabbi in front of the congregation.

What is the custom of going to the *mikveh*?

In more traditional communities, a Jewish woman goes to the *mikveh,* the ritual bath, within four days of the wedding ceremony. She does this to purify herself spiritually as she prepares for the transition to married life, and as a statement of the new relationship to be established between herself and her soon-to-be husband, or between two partners. Some married women will go to the *mikveh* once a month, in observance of the family purity laws (*taharat hamishpachah*), seven days after their menstrual flow has ceased, to be purified so that sexual relations may be resumed.

Today, many women are going to the *mikveh* as a way of creating a meaningful and spiritual passage from one stage of life to another. You may wish to speak with your rabbi or cantor about going to the *mikveh* prior to your wedding or to explore how you, as a woman, can spiritually enhance this moment.

Are there any prohibited days for a wedding?

Yes. A marriage cannot take place on certain days of the year for a variety of reasons. A wedding may not be held on Shabbat, because traditionally one cannot conduct business on the Sabbath and one does not take away from the joy of the Sabbath for another joy. For the latter reason, two members of the same family typically are not married on the same day.

Certain festivals and observances in the Jewish calendar prohibit marriages from taking place:

- The forty-nine-day period between Pesach and Shavuot, with the exception of four days (Lag BaOmer, the two days of Rosh Chodesh, and Yom HaAtzma-ut). These days reflect the forty-nine-day period that the Israelites waited between the Exodus from Egypt to the receiving of the Ten Commandments at Mount Sinai.

- The three-week period in the summer from the seventeenth of Tammuz to Tishah B'Av.

- Any of the three fast days, Holy Days, and festival days.

More liberal congregations will obviously have a more liberal interpretation and may not follow all of these restrictions. You will have to check with your particular congregation to make sure the date on which you wish to be married does not fall on one of the prohibited days.

Are there any prohibited partners?

Yes, if one is to adhere to a strict interpretation of teachings, there are restrictions as to who can marry whom. Men who can trace their ancestry back to the High Priest families of biblical times *(kohanim)* are prohibited from marrying widows and divorcees. Close family members cannot marry each other. Some scientists believe that intermarriage in families caused some of the Jewish genetic diseases. On the opposite side of prohibitions for a partner, there is the encouragement of Jews marrying Jews.

Why do the bride and groom fast before the wedding?

Traditionally, the bride and groom fast before the wedding as a way of marking this passage from one stage of life to another. The fast is not only for purification of the body, but of the soul as well. They pray and ask forgiveness for any wrong-doing they may have committed, beginning their life together on a "clean slate." There is always a word of caution for fasting brides and grooms, as there have been incidents of fainting under the *chuppah* due to lack of nourishment, so make sure that if you fast, you do so with extreme care.

What is the *bedeken* (veiling) of the bride?

Scholars relate this custom to the marriage of Leah to Jacob. Jacob believed he was to be wed to Rachel, the younger sister. Instead Laban, the father of the two sisters and Jacob's uncle, substituted the older sister, Leah, because it was the custom to marry the older sister first. Therefore, to be sure that the bride is his, the groom checks under the veil before the ceremony. The veiling is more recently interpreted as a statement of modesty, and a blessing is said over the bride during the *bedeken* ceremony.

What are the *Sheva B'rachot?*

The rabbi or cantor recites the *Sheva B'rachot* (Seven Blessings) during the marriage ceremony. These blessings seem to have their origin in the Talmud, where they are referred to as *Birkat Chatanim* (the Blessing of the Bridegrooms). Traditionally, the *Sheva B'rachot* are also recited at the feast following the ceremony. In the Seven Blessings, the first blessing is over the marriage cup of wine. The second and third blessings are in praise of God, who created nature and humankind. The next three are for the bridal couple. The last is a blessing for the couple, the community, and Israel. Following the Seven Blessings, the couple drink from the wine cup together.

What is *yichud?*

Yichud means "privacy" or "seclusion." At the end of the marriage ceremony, the couple enters a private room and breaks the fast together. As well, it is an opportunity for them to have a brief, quiet moment together to absorb the meaning of this important step and to share their joy. Following this encounter, the bride and groom rejoin their guests at the wedding festivities. A traditional period of *yichud* is not practiced in most Reform congregations.

Having a Family: Choices

- If you decide to have children, how will you afford a child? Will you wait until you have put money away? Will you make the economic adjustments necessary to have a child? Do you both agree?

- What about your careers? Will one of you leave your job? Will you leave permanently or take a temporary leave? What about child care? Day care or at-home caregiver? Who will be available in case of emergencies? How will you share in the responsibilities of caring for the children? Will one of you put your career on hold? How do you think you feel about that? Do you both agree with the solution?

- How do you feel about children? Will you have children only because it is expected? Do you have a deep desire for children? Are you prepared for what comes with having a child? Are you afraid to be a parent? Do you both share the same feelings or understand each other's feelings?

- Are you realistic about having children? Have you set up unrealistic goals for your children already? Can you accept a child that is not "perfect"? Are you prepared for how your life will change?

- How do you feel about the possibility of making financial adjustments?

The decision to have, or not have, children is not always made with just your own concerns in mind. There are social and peer pressures. Your parents and in-laws may pressure you to have children for their own needs. Friends may have children already and want you to share in the experience with them. Before you have made your decision regarding having children, try to be honest with yourselves and each other about your reasons for making this very important decision.

Remember, having a family is very rewarding, but parenting is hard work and requires commitment. Make sure that both of you are prepared to put in the time to raise healthy, well-adjusted children who are guided by the spiritual and moral beliefs of their tradition and their families.

Rabbi Elliot Dorff (in *This Is My Beloved, This Is My Friend: A Rabbinic Letter on Intimate Relations*, New York: The Rabbinic Assembly, 1996) offers us the following perspective:

> Children are not only an obligation: they are a blessing. Parents inevitably worry about their children, get angry with them on occasion, and experience their frustration and missteps together with them, but parents also share in their accomplishments and renew their own sense of the joy of life through them.
>
> Moreover, children are our destiny, perhaps our strongest tie to the future. Biblical and rabbinic sources affirm that . . . the influence we have had on others during our lifetime continues after our death, but we also . . . live on through our children. We are, after all, linked to the generations, both past and future, and children are one primary form of that bond.

The decision whether or not to have children is yours to make together. Within the liberal Jewish community, the sacredness of a union is not dependent on the couple's decision, or their ability, to procreate. In modern society, there are no clear-cut models for a family. We have many options and opportunities. One may make meaningful contributions to society without parenting.

Facts about Infertility

Infertility is an age-old problem. Jewish biblical stories, from Sarah to Rachel to Hannah, show each woman's long struggle with childlessness. These courageous women had to find alternatives. Sarah has her handmaid act as a surrogate; Rachel uses mandrakes as an aphrodisiac; Hannah prays for the gift of a child and promises to relinquish him as a priest. Our tradition offers much insight and perspective on infertility. Infertility can be a challenge for a couple. Being able to communicate with your partner about your hopes, fears, and disappointments regarding infertility is an important aspect of overcoming the anxiety that infertility can create for both partners. Consulting with a rabbi can be helpful to some couples, as well as counseling and appropriate medical intervention, should this be necessary.

Jewish Genetic Disorders

It is important that you become familiar with genetic diseases that affect individuals of Jewish descent and to know that genetic diseases occur among most ethnic, racial, and demographic groups. The genetic diseases discussed here occur more frequently in individuals of Ashkenazi Jewish ancestry, with the exception of familial dysautonomia, which may occur among individuals of other ethnic backgrounds, and the disease beta-thalassemia, which occurs in Jews of Sephardic descent. Most of these diseases are severely incapacitating and debilitating, many leading to death in infancy or early childhood.

Request a pamphlet on these diseases and their origins, published by the National Foundation for Jewish Genetic Diseases (**www.nfjd.org**; phone: 212-371-1030), which supports research and provides information to the public and the medical community about these diseases. The pamphlet describes in detail the nine most common genetic diseases, the nature of the defects, major symptoms, the diseases' course, diagnostic tests (including prenatal diagnosis and carrier detection), and available disease management and treatment.

The nine most common Jewish genetic diseases are Bloom's syndrome, Canavan disease, familial dysautonomia, Fanconi anemia, Gaucher disease, mucolipidosis IV, Neimann-Pick disease, Tay-Sachs disease, and torsion dystonia.

Many rabbis and physicians suggest genetic consultation prior to marriage. This may include an assessment of your family history and and testing for Tay-Sachs and possibly other genetic diseases. It is also advisable that individuals considering marriage be tested for the HIV-AIDS virus, even though this is not a genetic disorder.

Exercise 18. Mediating Differences in Jewish/Religious Backgrounds and Expectations for the Home

Write down some of your own personal reflections in response to the following questions.

1. What were some of your significant Jewish /religious experiences growing up?

2. How will these experiences impact on your decisions for the practice of Judaism/religion in your own home?

3. How will you decide together what model you will choose? Will you create your own? Paint a picture of your religious rituals and holidays in your home.

4. Who was a Jewish/religious role model for you? Why?

5. What role will this person play in your own home?

6. Has your role model, or lack of one, affected your own identification as a Jew in any significant way? If you are marrying out of your faith, how will that affect both your attitude and your decisions regarding Jewish or other religious traditions and rituals in the home?

7. Discuss spirituality in the context of your home.

At-Home Exercise

בָּרוּךְ אַתָּה, יְיָ אֱלֹהֵינוּ, מֶלֶךְ הָעוֹלָם, אֲשֶׁר בָּרָא שָׂשׂוֹן וְשִׂמְחָה, חָתָן וְכַלָּה, גִּילָה, רִנָּה, דִּיצָה וְחֶדְוָה, אַהֲבָה וְאַחֲוָה, שָׁלוֹם וְרֵעוּת. מְהֵרָה, יְיָ אֱלֹהֵינוּ, יִשָּׁמַע בְּעָרֵי יְהוּדָה וּבְחוּצוֹת יְרוּשָׁלַיִם קוֹל שָׂשׂוֹן וְקוֹל שִׂמְחָה, קוֹל חָתָן וְקוֹל כַּלָּה, קוֹל מִצְהֲלוֹת חֲתָנִים מֵחֻפָּתָם וּנְעָרִים מִמִּשְׁתֵּה נְגִינָתָם. בָּרוּךְ אַתָּה, יְיָ, מְשַׂמֵּחַ חָתָן עִם-הַכַּלָּה.

Baruch atah, Adonai Eloheinu, Melech haolam, asher bara sason v'simchah, chatan v'chalah, gilah, rinah, ditzah v'chedvah, ahavah v'achavah, shalom v'rei-ut. M'heirah, Adonai Eloheinu, yishama b'arei y'hudah uv'chutzot y'rushalayim kol sason v'kol simchah, kol chatan v'kol kalah, kol mitzhalot chatanim meichupatam un'arim mimishteih n'ginatam. Baruch atah, Adonai, m'samei-ach chatan im hakalah.

We praise You, *Adonai* our God, Ruler of the universe, Creator of joy and gladness, bride and groom, love and kinship, peace and friendship. O God, may there always be heard in the cities of Israel and in the streets of

Jerusalem: the sounds of joy and of happiness, the voice of the groom and the voice of the bride, the shouts of young people celebrating, and the songs of children at play. We praise You, *Adonai*, our God, who causes the bride and groom to rejoice together.

Seventh Blessing *(Sheva B'rachot)*

Blessing Exercise

(This exercise is to be done in class.)

Blessings abound as you plan for your life together.

1. Write a blessing for the joy of experiencing these weeks with other couples.

2. Create a blessing for members of the group for the homes they will be creating.

3. Create a blessing for yourselves that you may share now and in the future, reminding you of the joy you are feeling today.

This is the final session. If you wish to pursue your dialogue on the creation of your Jewish home, please refer to Rabbi Daniel Judson and Rabbi Nancy Wiener, *Meeting at the Well,* chapter 7.

Legal
Information

Read this information before Session 5. If you have specific questions, you should consult your lawyer or your state government offices. Laws change and circumstances differ, and important decisions should be based on the most current and accurate sources.

Your marriage and the partnership agreement into which you enter are of concern to both of you and perhaps your families, but it is also of concern to the state in which you reside. Each state has laws that govern several aspects of your marriage, including but not limited to property. You should know what the law says about marriage.

Please note: It is important to check with your lawyer or government officials before making legal decisions. Laws change, and you need to be aware of their impact on your decisions. Gay and lesbian couples can consult **www. vtfreetomarry.org** and **www.chavizedek.com**; both sites offer information on changes in the law regarding marriage and the granting of marriage rights to couples.

- Marriage between parties of sufficient age and mental capacity to contract is a common right, but this common right does not extend to marriages that are incestuous, polygamous, or perhaps where prohibited by a decree of divorce.

- Marriages between immature minors are unlawful. Age eighteen has been set as the age of consent, where full status is achieved to enter into marriage.

- Marriage between two parties must be by mutual intent and agreement or the consent of both parties.

- All persons intending to marry must obtain a marriage license, and that license must be delivered to the officiating clergyman or magistrate.

However, if both parties are of full age, the marriage is not invalidated by the fact that they have not obtained a marriage license.

- Since the enactment of amendments to the Domestic Relations Law and the Civil Rights Law of 1985, women are no longer obligated to adopt the surname of their husband. In fact, any person has the right to adopt any name by which he/she wishes to be known. Parties to a marriage need not have the same last name.

- In the case of a second marriage, a marriage license may not be issued if an applicant has been previously married, his or her spouse is still living, and such marriage has not been terminated by any decree of a court of competent jurisdiction, unless the applicant establishes the invalidity of such a first marriage.

  Where an application shows that an applicant has been previously married, but that a court of another jurisdiction has terminated the marriage, the validity of a foreign decree of divorce must be inquired into by the clerk. If it appears that the foreign court was without jurisdiction over the parties to the divorce action, the license may not be issued. The burden of proof is upon the applicant, but the burden to prove the foreign court was without jurisdiction is upon the clerk.

- A ceremony that is solemnized by a clergyman or magistrate need not take any particular form so long as the parties solemnly declare in the presence of a clergyman or magistrate and the attending witness or witnesses that they take each other as husband and wife. The license having been legally issued, the marriage may be solemnized in any location.

- A clergyman or minister of any religion, recognized by his/her church as such, is authorized to solemnize a marriage, and it is not necessary that he/she be ordained. In addition, one who has performed the services of a rabbi or cantor, and is known to his/her congregation as such, may solemnize a marriage, even though there is no evidence that he/she was ever authorized by any governing body to act as rabbi/cantor. A nonresident clergyman or minister may perform a marriage ceremony.

What is listed below is based on New York State law. State law has a role in many facets of your impending marriage because it is a legal contract. It is important to remember that there are differences among states and provinces; however, there are some generalizations that seem consistent and they are listed below.

The nature of the marital relationship is known by ethical, moral, and religious standards as well as civil standards. It is equally important to understand the civil implications of your upcoming marriage as it is the ethical/religious/emotional and legal aspects. The following outlines the nature of marriage, as recognized by the state (these are New York State statutes):

1. Marriage is a civil status created by the legal union of a man and woman as husband and wife, which imposes certain duties and responsibilities toward each other and society for their joint lives until death or legal termination of the relationship.

2. Marriage is contractual by nature. However, it is distinguished from other types of contracts in the following manner:

   a. Marriage creates a status as well as imposing rights and duties upon parties to the marriage contract.

   b. Marriage is more restrictive by nature than other types of contracts due to the limitations imposed upon persons with respect to their capacity to enter into the marriage contract.

   c. Marriage generally requires a lesser degree of mental capacity than many other contractual situations.

   d. Marriage is permanent unless dissolved by a court of competent jurisdiction and, therefore, cannot be revoked at the will of the parties to the marriage contract.

   e. Marriage creates certain rights, which cannot be assigned, alienated, or transferred.

   f. Remedies for breach of marriage contract differ from the remedies available to the parties for breach of other types of contract.

   g. Marriage does not fall within the meaning of the constitutional prohibition against the impairment of contracts by the legislature.

3. The differences between marriage contracts and other types of contracts generally arise from the fact that marriage is an institution upon which the "family," an integral unit in modern society, is considered to be of vital importance to the state. Due to the significance of marriage to society and the parties, the state attempts to foster and protect the marriage relationship through its courts.

4. Due to its unique characteristics, it can be said that marriage is practically a contract among three parties: the man, the woman, and the state.

5. Traditional rules have related to marriages of members of the opposite sex. In recent years homosexuals and lesbians have attempted to marry members of

the same sex. They have challenged the state statutes that required the marriage to be between members of the opposite sex. However, courts have held that it is not a denial of the fundamental right to marry to require that the marriage be between persons of the opposite sex.

As well, if there are children, your responsibilities include the following:

1. To provide for the child's emotional care and stability.

2. To provide and maintain a loving, stable, consistent, and nurturing relationship and home environment.

3. To provide supervision and guidance for the child.

4. To protect the child's emotional, intellectual, moral, and spiritual development.

5. To provide and exercise appropriate judgment regarding the child's welfare, including the daily needs of the child, i.e., feeding, clothing, physical care and grooming, health care, and day care, and engaging in activities that are appropriate to the development level of the child and within the social and economic circumstances of your family.

6. To provide state-mandated education for the child.

7. To provide encouragement and protection of the child's moral and intellectual development, including remedial education.

8. To assist the child in developing and maintaining appropriate interpersonal relationships.

9. To provide financial security and support for the child in addition to child support obligations.

10. To be responsible for the child's torts (harmful actions).

11. To be responsible for the child's debts.

12. Not to be abusive or neglectful of the child.

You have rights:

1. The law acknowledges that the homemaker's role is equal to that of the breadwinner, if the family is not a dual-income family.

2. Neither partner may abuse the other.

3. Adultery is against the law.

The following are laws regarding the accumulation of property:

1. Marital property is everything that has been garnered since the marriage, i.e., real estate, stocks, bonds, 401Ks, IRAs, defined pension plans, silver, crystal, china, art, copyrights, patents, coin collections, etc.

2. If your state has a community property law, then all property accumulated by the spouses either jointly or individually becomes property owned equally by the parties.

3. Separate property is what you bring into the marriage (gifts, inheritances), though enhancement of separate property may become marital property.

Resources

General Jewish Resources

Union for Reform Judaism, 633 Third Avenue, New York, New York 10017, **www.urj.org**

Central Conference of American Rabbis, 355 Lexington Avenue, New York, New York 10017, **www.ccarnet.org**

The URJ Press publishes books and learning materials from a wide spectrum of authors and subjects. Their catalog of titles is available on-line at: **www. urjpress.org.**

Reform Judaism Magazine, 633 Third Avenue, New York, New York 10017

www.myjewishlearning.com includes a rich variety of engaging, well-written, and easily accessible content appropriate for visitors of diverse backgrounds and levels of Jewish knowledge.

www.jewishlights.com includes a complete catalog of this publisher's adult and children's books on spirituality, Jewish practice, theology philosophy, and more.

Books

Jewish Practice and Wedding

Diamant, Anita. *The New Jewish Wedding Book.* Fireside: New York 1993.

Einstein, Steve, and Lydia Kukoff. *Introduction to Judaism: A Source Book.* New York: UAHC Press, 1999.

Heschel, Abraham Joshua. *The Sabbath*. New York: Noonday Press, 1996.

Heschel, Abraham Joshua. *God in Search of Man*. New York: Noonday Press, 1997.

Holtz, Barry. *Back to the Sources*. New York: Touchstone Books, 1986.

Judson, Rabbi Daniel, and Rabbi Nancy Wiener. *Meeting at the Well*. New York: UAHC Press, 2002.

Stern, Chaim. *On the Doorposts of Your House: Prayers and Ceremonies for the Jewish Home*. New York: CCAR Press, 1994.

Strassfeld, Michael. *Jewish Holidays*. New York: HarperCollins, 1985.

Syme, Daniel. *The Jewish Home*. New York: UAHC Press, 2003.

Washofsky, Mark. *Jewish Living: A Guide to Contemporary Reform Practice*. New York: UAHC Press, 2001.

Wiener, Nancy H. *Beyond Breaking the Glass: A Spiritual Guide to Your Jewish Wedding*. New York: CCAR Press, 2001.

On Marriage

Crohn, Joel, Howard J. Markman, Susan L. Blumberg, and Janice R. Levine. *Fighting for Your Jewish Marriage: Preserving a Lasting Promise*. San Francisco: Jossey-Bass, 2000.

Gottman, John M., Ph.D., and Nan Silver. *The Seven Principles of Making Marriage Work*. New York: Crown, 1999.

Gottman, John M., Ph.D., and Nan Silver. *Why Marriages Succeed or Fail*. New York: Fireside, 1994.

For Interfaith Couples

Cowan, Paul, and Rachel Cowan. *Mixed Blessings: Marriage Between Jews and Christians*. New York: Doubleday, 1987.

Glaser, Gabrielle. *Strangers to the Tribe.* New York: Houghton Mifflin, 1997.

King, Andrea. *If I'm Jewish and You're Christian, What Are the Kids?* New York: UAHC Press, 1993.

Petsonk, Judy, and Jim Remsen. *The Intermarriage Handbook: A Guide for Jews and Christians.* New York: William Morrow, 1988.

Schneider, Susan Weidman. *Intermarriage: The Challenge of Living with Differences Between Christians and Jews.* New York: The Free Press, Macmillian Publishing Co., Inc., 1989.

Reference

Etz Hayim: A Torah Commentary. Edited by David L. Lieber, et al. Philadelphia: Jewish Publication Society, 2002.

Encyclopaedia Judaica.

The Torah: A Modern Commentary. Edited by W. Gunther Plaut. New York: UAHC Press, 1981.

The Jewish Home

Holtz, Barry. *Back to the Sources.* New York: Touchstone Books, 196.

Syme, Daniel. *The Jewish Home.* New York: URJ Press, 2004.

Gay and Lesbian Resources

Kah, Yoel. *Kiddushin: Union Ceremonies for Gay and Lesbian Jews.* San Francisco: Congregation Sha'ar Zahav, 1994.

"The Kedushah of Homosexual Relationships." *CCAR Yearbook* 99 (1989): 136–145.

"Same Sex Marriage in Our Generation." *New Menorah Journal* 59 (spring 5760/2000). Includes the following articles: "Learning about Homosexuality and Taking a New Stand" by Elliot N. Dorff; "Premarital Counseling" by Rabbi

Nancy H. Wiener; "Legal Protection" by Susan Saxe; "Honor the Holiness of Lesbian and Gay Marriages" by Rabbi Sue Levi Elwell; "A Covenant of Same-Sex Nisu'in and Kidushin" by Eyal Levenson; "Gay Marriage—What's the Fuss?" by Susan Saxe; "Same-Sex Marriage and the Law" by Rabbi Rebecca Alpert; "A 'Becoming' of a New Sexual Ethic" by Rabbi Arthur Waskow.

Domestic Violence Resources

National Domestic Violence Hotline: 1-800-799-SAFE

National Child Abuse Hotline: 1-800-4-A-CHILD

www.jewishwomen.org

Jewish Women International, 1828 L St. NW, Suite 250, Washington, DC 20036; phone: (202) 857-1300; jkarotkin@jwi.org

Shalom Task Force, P.O. Box 3028, Grand Central Station, New York, NY 10163; hotline: (718) 337-3700. Provides a bibliography of resources dealing with sexual and domestic violence in the Jewish community.

www.mncava.umn.edu/bibs/jewish.htm

JewishFamily Services

Associationof Jewish Family and Children's Agencies, 557 Cranbury Rd., Suite 2, East Brunwick, NJ 08816-5419; phone: 1-800-634-7346; www.ajfca.org

Interfaith Support and Outreach

Jewish Outreach Institute, Center for Jewish Studies, 365 Fifth Ave., New York, NY 10016; phone: (212) 817-1952; www.joi.org

Adoption

Stars of David International, Inc., www.starsofdavid.org

Department of Jewish Family Concerns

Mission Statement

Within the Reform Jewish community, our families are ever more diverse and are increasingly confronted with complex health, social, and human service needs. Together, individuals and families who had historically been marginalized by the Jewish community now look increasingly to their faith for response. Most importantly, they look to their synagogue community for support and understanding.

URJ synagogues are working to be places where all can comfortably come to worship, sing, celebrate, mourn, and grow. To turn a synagogue into a fully inclusive and caring community, however, can often be a daunting task. The Department of Jewish Family Concerns works to help congregations make the transition into caring communities. The department also helps congregations to create their own Caring Community/Family Concerns committees and programs.

Caring Communities

"The Caring Community" programs are designed as "inreach" to hospital visitation, bereavement groups, and the development of support networks for a wide variety of needs. This committee has prepared the publication *Creating a Caring Community/Family Concerns Committee Within Your Congregation,* designed to introduce you and your committee members to basic ideas to get your program off the ground.

To receive a copy of this publication or for individual consultation on how to create a caring community, please contact the Department of Jewish Family Concerns.

Jewish Family Concerns cosponsors a team training program for clergy and lay leaders, The Synagogue as a Center for Healing and Caring. Workshops in *bikur cholim,* spiritual support groups, healing liturgy, and understanding and working with people in grief are offered.

HIV and AIDS

Jews with AIDS have prayers both to offer and receive. The Jewish community has, at times, fallen victim to society's widespread fears and prejudices toward people who have the virus. Even in congregations where goodwill prevails, outreach, inclusion, and support for Jewish families confronted by HIV/AIDS can seem overwhelmingly complex and fraught with discomfort. Some of the issues HIV/AIDS has forced us to confront—sexuality, sexual relations, drug abuse, and condom usage—leave Jewish communities searching for a true foundation of acceptance and sensitivity.

The Department of Jewish Family Concerns works to ensure that congregations are welcoming and caring environments where those who have contracted HIV/AIDS can offer and receive prayers.

Gay and Lesbian Inclusion

The committee on Gay and Lesbian Inclusion works with congregations and communities to develop a more welcoming, inclusive culture. We have resources to help, including referrals to local organizations, liturgy appropriate for a variety of communities, and *Kulanu,* our program guide for congregations implementing gay and lesbian inclusion.

Kulanu is a complete primer suited for any congregation or community that is trying to become more open and welcoming, whatever stage of that process it may be in.

Lehiyot: Special Needs

Access to Judaism has been a hallmark of the Reform Movement since our first congregation began seating women and men together over 120 years ago. Today, access involves such things as large-print prayer books, sign interpretation at services, bar and bat mitzvah training for children with special needs, and increasing sensitivity to the scope of needs within each community.

The Department of Jewish Family Concerns helps congregations create and enhance inclusive environments and accessible spaces to ensure that everyone is included. Every congregant has a right to a rich Jewish life in a welcoming environment.

Older Adults: The Graying of Our Congregation

In the not-too-distant future, one-fifth of the Jewish population of North America will be over sixty-five, with the greatest percentage increase being among those over eighty-five. These older adults are turning to their Jewish community to enrich their lives.

The Department of Jewish Family Concerns works with congregations to provide meaningful programming, life-passage rituals, and enhanced support for these individuals. Increased longevity creates new challenges for our community. Soon, the "children of the sixties" will reach *their* sixties. Just as these midlifers' children reach independence, the demands of their elderly parents pull their energies back to caregiving, casting them as the "sandwich generation."

Pulled in many directions, these midlifers turn to their Jewish community for support. The Department of Jewish Family Concerns works with congregations to ensure that the Reform Jewish community provides for and learns from our older generations.

Yad Tikvah: Preventing Self-Destructive Behaviors

Adolescence, one of the most stressful periods in life, is both turbulent and exciting. New opportunities as well as new dangers seem to be around every corner. For our young people, for their parents and families, and for their Jewish communities, coping with these challenges can be a challenge in itself.

For some of our youth, these challenges can lead to a feeling of hopelessness and isolation. When this hopelessness becomes dangerous, recognizing the warning signs is crucial. Since suicide and other forms of self-destructive behavior affect Jewish children and teens just as much as they affect the rest of the population, it is important to employ skilled methods of intervention. Self-destructive behaviors such as drugs, alcohol, and eating disorders affect not only individuals and families, but entire communities as well. No community needs to feel helpless in the face of statistics.

The Department of Jewish Family Concerns provides *Yad Tikvah,* or "Hand of Hope," an umbrella of programmatic responses for congregations to help families struggling with self-destructive behaviors.

To receive publications and resources concerning any of these programs, please contact: The URJ Department of Jewish Family Concerns, 633 Third Avenue, New York, NY 10017, Phone: (212) 650-4294; fax: (212) 650-4239, **jfc@urj.org**; **www.urj.org/jfc.**